THE
BIG
FIX

Praise for **THE BIG FIX**

"*The Big Fix* is wonderfully powerful. Tracey Mitchell's transformative journey from the utter misery of heroin addiction to her hard-earned struggle to get and stay sober against all odds is one of the best memoirs I've read in years. Mitchell is a remarkably strong woman with a remarkably strong story of renewal, hope, and redemption."

—James Brown, author of *The Los Angeles Diaries*

"Tracey Helton went from street junkie, hooking for heroin, to wife, mother of three, and PTA treasurer—a tale of one woman's rise out of despair and enslavement to find self-reliance, joy, and hope. As we face repairing the wreckage caused by our nationwide opiate scourge, her story is one so many Americans now need to hear."

—Sam Quinones, journalist and author of *Dreamland: The True Tale of America's Opiate Epidemic*

"Heroin is a journey into darkness. Tracey Helton Mitchell tells the vivid and inspiring story of how she found her way to sunlight . . . Tracey is a remarkable individual who's written a vivid, honest, and moving book about addiction, courage, and hope."

—Steven Okazaki, Academy Award–winning filmmaker of *Black Tar Heroin* and *Heroin: Cape Cod, USA*

TRACEY HELTON MITCHELL

THE BIG FIX

HOPE AFTER HEROIN

SEAL

Published by Seal Press,
an imprint of Perseus Books, LLC,
a subsidiary of Hachette Book Group, Inc.
1700 Fourth Street
Berkeley, California
sealpress.com

ISBN: 9781580056632 (paperback)

Library of Congress Cataloging-in-Publication Data
Mitchell, Tracey Helton
ISBN 9781580056038
Mitchell, Tracey Helton. | Women drug addicts--United
    States--Biography. | Drug addicts—Rehabilitation—United
    States--Biography. | Heroin abuse-—United States.
LCC HV5805.M57 A3 2015
DDC 362.29/3092--dc23

10 9 8 7 6 5 4 3 2 1

Cover design by Tim Green, Faceout Studio
Interior design by Tabitha Lahr

Dedicated to the memory of my mother

CONTENTS

PART ONE

MY STORY

Like many Americans, my road to addiction started with a trip to a medical professional. At seventeen, I got my first taste of opioids after my wisdom teeth were extracted. I was a talkative yet very shy teenager, so my exposure to drugs had been limited to the small world around me, mainly my older siblings. Witnessing them in their experimentation phases had made me keenly aware of how silly a person on weed or alcohol could act. I had tried both of those substances a few times myself. I found neither to be all that appealing. But those white pills—they seemed like magic. I remember all the troubles of the world slowly melting away into a pool of euphoria. Little did I know, I would spend eight years of my life chasing that feeling on a daily basis.

Fast forward to a few years later. I had been imagining a way to return to that feeling. How could I get access to those magical pills? I wondered about acquiring some as I entered the hurried world of university life. It didn't take long until I found a solution through friends. Their parents had pills on hand—from injuries, from surgeries, and from medical procedures that had healed long ago. They had forgotten about those bottles in their medicine cabinets. When you moved aside the cough medicine and the Q-tips, these glorious substances appeared from behind the hair gel as a beacon of hope. There they were! The picture showing the droopy eyes and the words MAY CAUSE DROWSINESS and DO NOT OPERATE MACHINERY signaled a good time was in our future.

The pills seemed the perfect enhancement to any night out. A few drinks, some pills, I was a happy woman. Sure, I lost some friends. That hardly mattered to me. I made new ones! I made better ones! I made friends who were not only accepting of my changing lifestyle, they encouraged it. They asked me if I wanted to try the needle. Injecting the pills would be the best use of my limited resources, they told me, after they worked some magic to separate out the binders and lick off the coating, and I held out my arm. I barely felt a thing. The first time wasn't much, nor the second. What was I missing? But after trying a few more times, I began to see the appeal. Pins and needles in my extremities. A numbness in my core. My appetite only increased with time until, finally, I graduated to Lady H.

Heroin was supposed to be the ultimate drug experience. I was completely unaware of the nature of the diminishing returns. No time is like the first time—it felt like the best orgasm, the best hug, and the warmest blanket all

wrapped up into a pile of *ahh yes!* I spent many years trying to recapture that feeling that soon slipped away from
me. My drug-induced confidence was quickly replaced with
anxiety. My painless days were followed by sleepless nights.
I lost everything that I hadn't already sold or traded for this
drug, until I was brought into my new life in handcuffs.

It would be misleading to imply that my recovery was
a linear process. It is true that once I made the decision to
stop using and enter recovery, I never relapsed. However,
there were many failures before there were many successes. I
would be remiss if I excluded the ten other times I had kicked
heroin, only to return to it. Let me outline my major attempts.
I quit drinking and drugs for six months at nineteen years
old. This was with just my "willpower." I had one painful
detox at home on my couch in Cincinnati. There were a few
months at a time when I swore off drugs before I moved to
San Francisco. I lived in a national park in Colorado for
almost a month in an attempt to quit hard drugs. There was a
twenty-one-day methadone detox. There were three different
times I kicked on my own—once while I was living on the
sidewalk, twitching and puking into the gutter. There were
two different times I was forced to kick heroin in jail, only
to return to drugs within hours of my release. Finally, there
were two weeks on methadone maintenance a month before
my final arrest.

I was also a polysubstance user who switched from drug
to drug, complicating my recovery. During the last few years,
I was using them all together, like a cocktail to celebrate my
destruction. Between extended periods of heavy drinking, cocaine use, and methamphetamine-fueled binges, heroin was

the thread that tied up my dysfunction into a not-so-pretty package. It wasn't "just" the heroin. The heroin was just my first and last crutch. I gave up all substances, including alcohol, to be free. That is my personal story.

I may not have stayed sober every time I tried, but I learned something from each attempt to get clean. By the time I went to jail for the last time on that foggy night in late February 1998, I was ready to put all my hard-earned knowledge into practice. With each passing minute, with each passing hour, with each passing day I got stronger for my attempts. No matter how many times you have tried in the past, you only need to get it right *one* time. I tell people seeking my assistance: Make NOW that time.

The process of getting clean was a road with many twists and turns. The brief summary of my recovery goes like this: jail, detox, rehab, sober living, twelve steps, support groups, and therapy. Those were the things that worked for me.

I didn't start my recovery thinking I would become an advocate for addicts; at first my focus was just on staying clean myself. But I have seen people change before my eyes when they hear my story and begin to believe recovery is possible. Many addicts say to me, "Tracey, you are such a role model." What do I say to them? Do I take the credit for the little bit of luck and the big portion of fear that have motivated me to stay clear of active addiction? Do I give advice when I feel as if I don't even have mastery of my own life and my own emotions? Generally, I am so humbled by the opportunity to help someone that it leaves me speechless, so all I can say is, "Thank you." Thank you for caring enough to take time out of your life to talk to me. I gain strength knowing that I can still contribute to a world when I spent so much time taking from everyone around me.

To some, my story, my journey to recovery, is a cautionary tale. To others, it is a light in the dark world known as addiction. When I look at the life I have built for myself, it is hard for even me to believe that I was ever a homeless drug addict. To this day, when I reflect on how I went from college student to junkie, I have more questions than answers. Could something have changed the trajectory of my life? I am not sure. Was I hooked from the very start? It is hard to say. These questions are impossible to answer. What I do know is when I hold my child's hand or help a person in need, all of the pain I suffered becomes transformative. I have learned from my journey that I am strong. I am capable of great things. Not despite my past, but because of it. To honor all those who have been lost to drugs and to avoid losing more, we must demand changes to our current policies. Don't be left wondering whether you could have done something to help the user in your life. We can all do something that will make a difference. I am the proof.

Chapter 1

THE OTHER SIDE

When I get to work this morning, I glance through the notifications on my phone and something unusual catches my attention. This is more than someone liking my picture on Instagram. This isn't telling me about a 15 percent off sale, if I can just drag myself into a hideously crowded store. This is something different. "I wanted to tell you that you saved my life. When I was . . ." Someone must have left a message on one of my profiles. Even though it seems like I have so many ways to connect with the world, there are still so many moments that are lonely. I often think about how addiction is the constant state of dissatisfaction and disconnection with the positive things in life. Many days, even without drugs, I still feel that state of unease. This phone, these messages, let me connect with others who understand. When I get a minute away from my desk, I'll sneak off to the bathroom to read the rest of the message. For now, I need to focus on getting myself together for a long day at the office.

My morning started off with the cat jumping on my head. He is really an asshole. I love him, of course, but his behavior can be intolerable even by cat standards. When that didn't wake me up, he stuck his paw in my eye. He is so mean that many people refuse to come over to my house—they are afraid of him. He reminds me of myself. He is sweet to those he loves, but is constantly on the defensive. We both are so afraid of being wounded, we end up spending a lot of time curled up in a ball, holding on for dear life. Anyway, apparently he thinks 5:02 AM is a perfect time to eat. I, on the other hand, wanted to savor my last twenty minutes in bed.

My night was filled with tossing and turning—otherwise known as the joy of perimenopause. I still cannot understand how I can be in perimenopause when my youngest is still in diapers. My relatively late-in-life third child reveals a whole other realm of my ironic life decisions. Having a toddler in my forties is exhausting. Not quite staying-up-for-three-days-on-cocaine exhausting, but exhausting nevertheless. When my three children get through college, I will be well into my sixties. But this is all part of a life I never imagined, much less planned. When I was young, I had dreamed of having a baby one day. Then I traded in that dream for a bag of heroin, and my plans changed to "live fast and die by thirty."

Who could have ever imagined me, the junkie whore, as a caring mother? Yet when I gave birth to my children, mothering came naturally to me. I will always remember them as my beautiful miracle babies snuggling with me in the hospital. They were the true gifts of my recovery, gifts beyond my comprehension. The joy I felt as a new mother was easily the highlight of my life. I suppose it also provided me with a dose of the happy chemicals I read about on the mothering forums. Nursing and cuddling with a child are supposed to provide oxytocin, which results in a warm and content emotional state. I suppose I have gotten attached to my natural baby high. Giving up nursing, that feeling of connection, as my children grow is bittersweet. When I formed this bond with my first child, it was as if I had run a marathon. I felt as if I had achieved the impossible. I had overcome addiction and created a new life. My children were the manifestation of that. Nurturing each child reminded me of how I had nurtured myself.

Not that it's always been easy. Given my history, I had to fight with medical providers when I wanted to nurse my baby. Nursing is the last link to joy-filled time after having a new baby. Even now, I'm still bitter over a thoughtless comment a nurse made when I'd just had my first child and she saw on my chart that I used to be an intravenous drug user.

"Are you sure this is okay?" she asked me.

I pretended not to hear her. I stroked the hair of my baby as I fed her. I drank in her smell. The smell of my new baby was more intoxicating than any drug combination I had put into my body. I experienced more love in that moment than I have ever felt through a needle. For a brief second, my life was complete. That empty pit in my heart I had filled with substances was gone. It was as if those ten years on drugs had been erased with the birth of my daughter. I was more than an addict. I was a powerful woman. Finally, I had created something good in the universe. When my daughter arrived in my arms, I was reborn.

She started again. "Are you sure you should be doing that?"

"What do you mean?" I asked, still half ignoring her.

Nurses were constantly coming in and out of my room, offering unsolicited advice. While the majority of the medical staff were helpful, it only took one to sour my experience.

She continued. "Are you sure you should be breastfeeding the baby with your history?"

I wanted to throw something across the room. Can't she see that I have changed? Can't this woman see that I'm a new person? The arrogance—on my part. I actually believed I could be a normal woman. I actually believed I could be accepted as something beyond my history. I ignored her again. She needed to get the fuck out of my room.

The buzz of the alarm interrupts me. I had turned over in hopes of getting five more minutes of sleep. I guess I slipped into a dream, or, really, a painful memory. My husband is already at work, long gone. He is a solid, hardworking man. He is the type of man who supports me while giving me the freedom to be myself. He works in construction, and I love him for his white T-shirts and blue jeans. He provides stability to balance out the crazy thoughts that run around in my mind. He loves me without judgment. I respect him, especially on a day like today. Many mornings, he leaves the house at 4:30 AM for the long commute to his jobs down the peninsula. I sometimes wonder how he can function with so little sleep.

I give myself exactly one hour to get ready in the morning. I have to feed myself, wake the kids, feed the kids, dress the kids, make my lunch, make their lunch, and get out the door without losing my shit. I wonder how many parents out there are also about to pull their hair out with stress. I find it strangely comforting when I see another family struggling with their children in my morning travels. When a mom has to pick her fitful toddler off the ground or I see a dad struggling with a stroller on the train, I give them an empathetic nod of recognition. I see you, weary warrior. Having children is hard work. So many things to do in the morning! It will be a miracle if I can do all of this without raising my voice. Two kids go off to the elementary school and one to daycare. Fortunately, I have some help with transporting the big kids to school.

I had a "little" incident a year or so ago when I had a panic attack while driving seventy miles an hour on the highway like a madwoman to get to the train station so I could get to work on time. I am not sure if it was the three and a half cups of coffee a day I drank to stay awake. Maybe I had just reached some type of mental mommy critical mass. The panic attack was an ugly scene that made me question the way I managed my life and my time. That was one of many breaking points. After that, I knew it was time to look for some new solutions. One of the gifts of my recovery is that I have learned to ask for help. One of the teachers at the school kindly agreed to drop off my older kids for less money than I spent on gas. That change makes my morning flow instead of coming to a screeching halt. I also cut back on the caffeine.

In the category of everyday miracles, both my trains were on time this morning. This makes me feel like the commuter equivalent of a rock star. I made it to work with a few minutes to spare this morning. In fact, my son cooperated every step of the way. I had the assistance of some snacks for minor bribes. The best part of not driving in the morning is I get a few extra cuddles with my son. As he sits next to me looking out the window, I bury my head in his hair. That sweet smell brings a smile to my face. The softness of his hand inside my hand can make being ten minutes late seem completely insignificant when it used to be everything. I used to practically have a mental breakdown if I was late. I was that irritating person who always showed up early for everything. Now, I feel satisfied if I arrive at all with clothes on that match. I am no longer just working harder, I am working smarter. Of my four years of business school, this seems to be the one thing I remember. For my own mental health, I need this time with my son. I deserve this time. When he waves goodbye to me, my heart breaks. Mothering time is over.

I snap back to my routine at my desk. In the middle of multitasking, my mind frequently wanders off. Fortunately, I seem to have some sort of muscle memory that can help me navigate even when I am on autopilot. I have so many things to cram into a single day. I come back into the moment in front of a white screen full of emails needing my attention. I have twenty minutes or so to stuff my face with yogurt and tea. Supposedly hydration is the key to balance. I find this amusing, since the only hydration I practiced before my thirties involved a syringe and a cotton for a filter. Now, here I am drinking tea by the fistful, waiting for the staff to start trickling in. Since today was a miracle day with *ten* whole extra minutes, I have time to look at my new message.

> *I saw the movie Black Tar Heroin: The Dark End of the Street in high school. The film had a huge impact on me. It only briefly stopped me from trying opiates at 20 years old. My boyfriend got me started with OxyContin and switched to heroin when oxy became too expensive. There is no harm reduction here, no treatment I can afford. After years in and out of jails and rehab, I have 32 days clean. I saw some of your videos. You are such an inspiration to me.*

The writer pleads with me to explain to her what I did to stay clean. I push myself back into my chair. I need to take a moment. When I read these kinds of messages, I try to knock all of the elements of my rational mind down a notch and let my emotions flood in. It would be really easy to provide a long list of clinical advice. First you need to do this, then that, and good luck to you. But that is not what this person is seeking. When people contact me, they want a connection. They saw me on the screen. They feel as if they know me. This person wants to connect with me, the addict. She wants to know what I did to put myself in that place again when I was struggling to keep the needle out of my neck. She doesn't want some rote catchphrases devised in rehab. She wants me to reflect and respond.

Her words make my heart ache. I know this pain. While thirty-two days is enough time to physically feel much better, the road to real restoration is a much longer path. When I look at her face in the compressed photo next to her name, I see myself at twenty-seven. She has that overly made-up face, a mask to deflect from her emotions. I remember standing at the mirror putting on eyeliner like it was somehow a ring that would hold back my tears. I caked foundation on my scars, applied lipstick to draw away from my chipped front tooth.

She sees me as a heroine.

To a generation of young people struggling with addiction, I am known as the heroine of heroin. The documentary this woman is referring to—*Black Tar Heroin*—featured me when I was a junkie in my mid-twenties. It was aired on HBO in 1998 and still has a cult following around the world. Articles have been written about me since then extolling the fact that I have done what seemed completely impossible: I have been clean since February 27, 1998. That makes an impression on anyone who knows anything about this drug. When I agreed to do the film, I thought I would soon be dead from an overdose or homicide and that my story would be no more than a cautionary tale that would live on long after I was gone. My story is now one of transformation. I have escaped what has killed so many others.

This young woman is reaching out to me for answers. I might have a few, but I'm not sure I can fully explain in a few sentences what has taken me so long to learn. I can try. I need to explain that recovery is a long process full of ups and downs. Getting off heroin is just the start. The real work comes after you put down the drugs. Heroin controls every element of your life. Heroin dictates your finances, your sex life, your family relationships, your mental health, your physical health, your spiritual condition.

I always take a few minutes to collect my thoughts before replying to such a thoughtful message. I reflect on the massive changes in my life since I stopped slowly poisoning myself. Why was I one of the few to get out of that life? Why was it me? What is it about me that made my story so different from that of hundreds of young people I knew who died in addiction? I was what is known as a low-bottom junkie. My using took me into horrors rarely witnessed, and rarely escaped.

I was using heroin during the era of AIDS. When a friend first pushed a needle into my arm, it was a used one. We would use the same needle—hoping it wouldn't break off in our arm—until the numbers on the side of the syringe wore off. Needle exchange programs and other services to assist users were nonexistent where I grew up in the Midwest. If you went to the hospital for an overdose or an infection, you could easily be taken to jail. People who had overdosed were dumped on the street, in hallways, or, if they were lucky, outside the hospital. A heroin user was considered to be the lowest of the low in society. We were told AIDS was cosmic retribution for our sins. The world would be a better place if we all just died off.

Heroin was expensive back then. The first time I tried it, I paid $30 for a bag that I split with another person. The bag started out at one-tenth of a gram. I have little doubt one of my friends dipped into the bag before I did. This was probably for the best. Recently one of our friends had overdosed and had to be revived, so everyone agreed I should only do half of that bag. "You can always do more," my friends said. "You can never do less." It was a "stamp" bag from New York City. It was engraved with 666. This should have been an omen. To me, it was a dream come true. After a year of planning it, I was finally going to try heroin.

I was cautious, afraid to put my life in the hands of another junkie who had agreed to inject me. My friend reminded me that this was something I had wanted to try for a long time. I held my breath, then motioned for my friend who had agreed to inject me to go ahead. It was exciting and terrifying at the same time, but nothing would stop me from experiencing the ultimate high.

Heroin was not widely available in the U.S. at the time—it took us months to find it. It was clustered mostly in larger cities like Chicago, Detroit, Philadelphia, New York City, and San Francisco. These cities had what are called open-air drug markets on street corners where heroin could be purchased. New York had storefronts that doubled as drug houses. A person could purchase a pack of gum and a bundle of heroin. My friends and I would travel to large cities to buy it and bring it back. When that ran out, we would go back to our normal routine—school, work, life—occasionally taking pills we stole from our parents. It was tough to have enough access to really get addicted. The first time I experienced any type of withdrawal, no one could tell me what was wrong with me.

The world in which this young woman lives now is entirely different from the one I left seventeen years ago.

Now heroin is readily available across most of the U.S. From the cities to the suburbs, heroin has penetrated most communities. If you have the funds, it can even be ordered off "dark market" sites on the Internet and shipped directly to your front door. Mexican cartels have been creating routes straight through the border to towns in the Midwest, where deaths from prescription drugs used to be king. As the government cracks down on legal opiates, users are turning to heroin as a less expensive substitute. This includes places like Cincinnati, near where I grew up. I went there recently for a benefit for their controversial new syringe exchange program. Users there reported to me that the streets are so flooded with heroin, dealers are known to hand out free samples to get new customers. Free samples! I am not sure I would have survived this current era.

Heroin has moved from the shadows into the living room. Somehow it has managed to become a more social experience. I hear about groups of high school students who started out stealing their parents' pills and end up railing lines of heroin together on the weekends during marathon Xbox sessions. When I started using heroin as a recreational user I was repeatedly told within social circles and by mere acquaintances that I was a "loser" and "ruining my life." Friends of mine were scolded by their friends for even associating with me. By the time I stopped using, many of these same people were asking me to get heroin for them. Heroin in social groups takes off like deadly dominoes, knocking people off one by one, until someone breaks the cycle. Users compare the process to making vampires: You hate the person who started you on the path, yet you find yourself creating new victims. That way you will not be so alone.

Heroin is now cheap, a ridiculous idea when I think of my twenty-two-year-old memories. With a few minor exceptions, heroin is cheaper in many places than a mixed drink at a bar or a pack of cigarettes. No more scrimping and saving and planning are necessary. A person can make a split-second decision to use that may change the course of his or her life. The woman who wrote me that message lives in a world where heroin is an option, not an exclusion. It isn't a struggle to get an affordable experience, one that has the potential for dire, unexpected consequences.

Heroin is also now extremely potent. In my using days, the heroin I was getting was tested at 20 to 38 percent pure. When street heroin would reach higher levels of purity, there were clusters of overdose deaths that followed. One nice lady in the cell next to me when I was in jail in 1996 had a brother who had died of an overdose, and she got a special overnight pass to attend his funeral. A few days later, the inmates received word she had also overdosed and died. A family was destroyed, taken by heroin in just a few days. Her son would no longer have a mother. But that was "heroin-lite" compared to what is now available to the young woman who wrote to me. Some samples recently tested on the East Coast are up to 70 percent pure.

I also did not have to worry about deadly additives like fentanyl back when I was using. Fentanyl, a synthetic opioid, looks like heroin but is much more potent. Clusters of users have been killed by the dozens across the U.S. when they unwittingly get a batch laced with this substance. There are so many risks, yet there are new users sampling heroin on a daily basis, trying to escape depression and anxiety, or just to get a taste of the euphoria that only this drug can deliver.

It takes a lot of courage to reach out to a stranger. As I think about what to say to this woman, I wonder what I could possibly say that might make a difference. I want to honor her confession. I have moved through the same dark tunnel out to the other side. To an observer, my life might seem removed from that place. It can now be quite ordinary. I have loads of laundry that need to be folded. I need to take the dog to get her shots. We just got *another* parking ticket for not moving the minivan on street-sweeping day. I have a pile of work on my desk. My to-do list is constantly over-flowing, like my toilet when my child stuffed it with a bunch of wet wipes.

What did I do to get my life back? I cannot sum it up in 140 characters on Twitter. I can't explain my process in just a few words. For people trying to hold on for their lives, the entirety of my story provides some answers. There is no quick fix when your drug of choice is heroin. I have searched for them. I would read elongated war stories about addiction. I would be curled up in a ball while I nibbled on a pint of ice cream. When I read these stories, I was still deep in the beating heart of drug addiction. I had the blood on my arms to prove it. As if by magic, the writer would get clean in the last chapter: "And now I have a fabulous life." The End. Or maybe the person died. Fuck. This wasn't helping me. It was the literary equivalent of a long sex session where your partner finishes, rolls over, and falls asleep. I lay there wanting more. I craved more. I needed more. I was looking for something I never really found. So I decided to create it.

I type out a couple sentences.

"Thanks so much for contacting me. Congrats on getting clean!" I stop. It feels as if the weight of the world is on my shoulders. Until the day I hit rehab, I never knew anyone who had gotten off drugs. I knew people who had died. Then there were some who went to prison. There were some who just disappeared one day. Clean was a rumor. Clean was a fairy tale. Clean was an island in the never-ending stream of depression and self-hatred. How could I get to that place? I wondered. Clean was so elusive, I was afraid to go there. It was impossible. They had to drag me into recovery in handcuffs. I was not sure I could ever change. That last time, I was willing to give it my best effort. Because I knew if I failed, the end result would be death.

This woman says she's thirty-two days off heroin. I admire her determination. Any day without a needle in your neck is a good day.

"The road in recovery is an uphill struggle, but well worth the energy," I tell her. "I am finally in a place in my life where I am willing to accept my imperfections. I don't need anyone or anything to fix me. I am okay in my own skin. It may take time to get there. Don't give up. You may not be able to replicate my process. Find what works for you."

I make a difference when I am willing to share my story. I know this to be true.

I turn my attention back to my work for the day. My

kids smile at me from my screen saver. Sixteen years ago I was dying on the streets of San Francisco. Now, I am the treasurer of the PTA. I take a breath to let it soak in. I take a moment to remember I am loved. Back to my keyboard.

Chapter 2

LET'S GET THIS OUT OF THE WAY: LIFE BEFORE RECOVERY

To understand what an uphill struggle it was for me to get to this place, you must first understand the road to my well-documented bottom. My first exposure to recreational drugs and alcohol came when I was growing up in the '70s. I had certainly been with teenagers smoking pot well out of view from their parents. I had heard all about Quaaludes, reds, blues, and other types of pills mentioned on the television shows of the day. But, as a nerdy teen, I spent most of my time focusing on my studies. I had taken a full load of Advanced Placement classes and was able to test out of nearly a full year of college coursework when I entered my freshman year. I barely dated until I reached my senior year of high school and didn't lose my virginity until almost my eighteenth birthday, with a boy I loved. My parents had no need to worry about me because on the surface I seemed to be the perfect child. I had smoked pot here and there. I had drunk a few beers. But I never drank alcohol for the taste. I only liked the effect. That should have been a clue that I should quit before I really got started.

I remember flipping through a magazine that talked about a drug called cocaine and how it was not addictive. A few years later, news reports told us crack was an "epidemic" sweeping the country. Still, during the Reagan era my parents must have felt that their three kids were well insulated from anything beyond a little excessive drinking or occasional use of "reefer," as my dad called it. We were only told to study hard and "just say no." To my parents, there was certainly little indication of what would become the beginning of my downward spiral.

When I moved out of my parents' home, it was as if a switch had been flipped. It was as if there had been a party going on my whole life, but I had never been invited until I got out on my own. I was always somewhere on a Friday or Saturday with a drink in my hand. Then there were little pick-me-ups to help the party last all night. When everyone was going to bed, I felt like I was just getting started. But I slowly dissolved into the woman who is always in the bathroom crying and angry at the world, eyeliner running down her face. The booze brought out the darker side of my personality.

Addiction slowly crept up on me, as it frequently does. It lied to me. It told me everything was okay. I can quit whenever I want. *See?* the inner addict told me. *You can go a few weeks or months without a drink. You have a job. You go to school. You can't possibly have a problem.* It wasn't hard to convince myself that everything I was doing was part of the college experience. Maybe that was true. Initially, drugs and alcohol were part of a social connection. As time went on, though, I found myself less and less interested in hanging out with friends and more and more interested in getting fucked up as my only goal. By the time I reached the age when I could legally go to bars, I was slowly becoming a shell of the person I was when I had left home a few years before.

By the time I turned twenty years old, my life had become a complicated mess where my moods were dictated by the presence or absence of substances. The struggle to maintain my fragile grip on sanity began the second I opened my eyes. Every day when I would wake up, my thoughts were always the same.

At least this time when I wake up it is morning. The last time I laid my head down, I believe it was in the afternoon. My internal clock is thrown off by the chemicals that pump through my veins.

"I hate my life," I mutter, as my eyes attempt to focus.

I say these words out loud frequently, with varying intensity depending on the mess I got myself into the night before. Today there is no one around to listen. But I don't need an audience or a witness to know my life is fucked. I am feeling grateful this morning that I didn't wake up half naked with some random person from the bar. I say "person" because my misery can be equal opportunity. I seem to drag people—both male and female—from all walks of life into my fuck-ups. The worst part for me is when I realize that some of these people have developed feelings for me. I don't want to lead them on. I bat my blue eyes, flip my hair, and whisper things they really want to hear. I should really find a way to take more psychology classes, study it full time. I suck people in with my ability to listen. In my black suede skirt and my ripped fishnet pantyhose, I may not be the prettiest woman in the bar, but I am the one who makes people want to sit with her and spill their deepest secrets. I am quite charming when I need something.

When I leave a bar, I begin an adventure in intoxicated navigation. My partner for the evening will often have to help me avoid running into yet another parking meter. I enjoy going over to other apartments, other places. There is generally a lack of food in my house. There is also a lack of companionship. I hate being alone, but I also hate being with someone. I am never satisfied. I always assume each of my companions is as drunk or high as I am, until one morning one of them is upset that I do not remember his name. Waking up alone in my own bed, today, is a relief. I hate that series of embarrassing questions when I wake up next to someone I don't really remember from the previous night. Where am I? Who are you? Where are my clothes? Trying to find my skirt and my shoes without waking them up has become my new survival skill. If they do wake up, they might want to cuddle. I am not into it. Definitely not the way I feel right now.

I cannot remember the last time I had sex with someone when I wasn't under the influence of something. Yet drugs have taken away my sex drive, my period, and most of my appetite. I guess I should be happy—no pesky pregnancy to worry about, I tell myself, although I am sure this is a lie. I remember those health classes where all the girls giggled in hushed tones. It wasn't that long ago that I was swishing around the hallway of my high school in my black watch plaid uniform skirt. *Why am I so smart yet make such dumb choices?* I ask myself. *Am I going to end up pregnant?* It could still happen. But since I have very little interest in anything beyond opiates and booze, I am not horny; I don't paw at my conquests to take me back to their place. Most of the time I cling to these unfortunate souls for survival. I am using them for drinks, or drugs, or a place close by to sleep. I am using them to help me navigate so I can make it home in one piece. Women get raped in these campus towns. I don't want that to happen to me. Sometimes, when they want to hold me, I wish I was capable of just loving them back. I wish I could be a person who succumbs to feelings. I can't do it.

Another day, another morning in agony. The first thing I try to do is move my hands. They are swollen like hard rocks. I slept with them resting on a pillow over my head at an angle that I hoped would make the swelling go down by morning. Gravity failed me last night, as it frequently does when I hit the curb drunk. My hands are swollen from letting a drunken companion dig into them way too many times with a needle. The alcohol and dope are long gone, but the damage remains. My fingers look like sausages. They are bruised around the knuckles—nerve damage from the needles—as if I'd been punching a wall. I try to use my hands to push myself up. Intense throbbing pain like razors slicing away at my flesh. There is no way I am going to make it to class today. I will be lucky if I can use these hands to wipe myself whenever I get the strength to go to the bathroom. My body feels as if a truck ran over me, backed up, and ran over me again.

What the fuck have I done this time? I think, as I catch sight of myself in the big piece of the broken mirror across the room. It was once a beautiful stand-up mirror until my friend Jeremy got drunk one night and decided to slit his wrists with it. I wasn't home at the time. I was on a beer run to Kentucky after the liquor stores in Ohio had closed. When I got back, I noticed the drops of blood on the floor before I saw this mess of a young man in the corner. Jeremy was nineteen years old with no ability to take care of himself. I am not sure if his parents had abandoned him, or exactly how he had ended up on the streets in such a small city. He was a beautiful creature with crystalline blue eyes that begged you to take him in. I had been letting him stay with me at my apartment. Two depressed alcoholics were one too many. I reached down to him.

"Jeremy," I said, "what have you done?"

He was in a near-catatonic state with cuts on his face and arms. He had deliberately broken my mirror, or knocked it over in a stupor. In the time it took for me to go get another case of beer, he had systematically cut up his face and forearms in slices that were, thankfully, superficial. There was blood, not a ton, but enough to let a person know a trauma had occurred. The biggest wound was on the inside. He had some type of broken psyche that led him to do these things over and over again. Now I knew why none of our friends wanted to let him stay over.

I was sad for a moment. Then I became angry, very fucking angry. I was angry that he had destroyed my things, though of course they could be replaced. I was angry that he had made a mess of my apartment, though that could be cleaned. I was angry that he couldn't see how much I cared for him, how much everyone loved him.

"Do you want blood?" I asked him.

I picked up a piece of mirror and sliced my own forearm. It was childish. It was stupid. In that moment, it was also effective. He got up to help me as the gash dripped blood onto the floor. I started crying. I was crying my eyes out as I reached to hold him. What could make a person who was so beautiful inside hate himself so much? I cried as I rocked him and begged him to never do something like this again. I cried so hard my eyes were swelling up as the blood crusted on my arm. I didn't care. Things were spinning out of control. He had to leave. He couldn't stay, and I couldn't keep him there.

Just like that morning after Jeremy left, today my eyes are slightly swollen. Puffy face—such a great look for me. The bags are creeping up like the rolling tide trying to squeeze my eyes closed. I really could use a drink of water. The sink is way too far away for me to manage at this point. Getting up is going to be a long process. Having a hangover would be more pleasant. At least I could clear that up with some puking and food. This is the aftermath of drugs.

The last four days have been a blur. I managed to get five days off in a row from my shitty retail job, and I got the "innocent" idea of a little binge to reward myself. I seem to have these binges more and more since Jeremy left for San Francisco. Now, I am hanging on by a thread to my "normal" life. I am struggling to drag myself up, here in my apartment across the street from the university campus. I suppose classes are going on right now. I haven't been there in a while. School is seriously getting in the way of my partying. I used to be able to snap back from these overindulgences so easily. As I get farther away from my friends and family, things seem to be getting harder and harder. I don't even know who I am anymore. This latest celebration started with a few shots at the bar and ended up with needle marks all over my hands.

There had been a slow transformation in my last few years of high school. As an overweight food addict, I had been on every diet possible. Finally, when I was sixteen, one diet stuck. I lost enough weight that people began to notice me as more than just the subject of ridicule. I began to feel differently about myself. Although I had hated being fat, fat was a place where I felt secure. Food provided me with a brief respite from my anger and anxiety. I shoved my feelings down with every bite. Then, after nearly a year of dieting, I was looking for something new to make me happy. Young men were a disappointing substitute. I tried writing poetry in notebooks that had stickers of my favorite bands peppering the covers. I started listening to punk rock music.

My neon purple sweaters switched to all black clothes. My Duran Duran poster soon sported the symbol for anarchy over the delicious eye of John Taylor. I was searching for my identity with little guidance and tons of confusion. Most of all, I was bored out of my skull preparing for college. I could not wait to get somewhere else so I could be someone besides myself.

If I smoked, now would be a good time for a cigarette. I hate reflecting on my behavior. Fuck that. I am not sure what else could help me get my day started. I look around at my scattered belongings. Where is my wallet? Surely it must be empty. I had just gotten my entire paycheck in cash at the corner store. There was no need to use a bank to cash it. My account is still overdrawn from the last time. My chain wallet is still attached to my pants, which are next to my mattress, which is on the floor. I never bothered to get a bed frame. That would just be something else to trip me in the middle of the night. I pull the wallet over to me. These hands can't open the snaps on the wallet. I use my teeth to open them. What is in here? Two dollars and a phone number written on a piece of paper. Who the fuck is this? I don't recognize the name. Some dealer, I am sure. The world starts spinning. Must be dehydration. The only water I get these days is drawn up with drugs in a syringe. *Ugh*. I'd better lie back down.

The throbbing in my hands is nearly unbearable. Why did I decide to binge like that? I got tired of spending my whole paycheck on mixed drinks every Friday night. Or on a bag of weed I would smoke up in one sitting. I needed something more. My friend at the bar told me he could get me some heroin. I hadn't had any for a while. I was getting scores from medicine cabinets here and there, but rarely could I get heroin. I was excited. I would need to wait until he got back from Dayton the next day, he had told me. He promised he would make it worth the wait. He leaned into me to let me know what he had in mind. I know he was just using me for my money. He had been a junkie in San Francisco before coming to this podunk town. He knew how to get what he wanted. So did I. I am sure the gin factored into my poor decision making when I told him yes.

The following day we were sitting on the floor of my apartment, where I trusted him to inject me in my hands with an old battered syringe. This was the only tool we had at our disposal. In fact, new syringes were so scarce, one couple I knew had spent an entire weekend hooked up to saline IVs so they had an open port to inject into. I had never even used a new syringe. I prepared the dull instrument. I had sharpened the needle on a matchbook in hopes that it would slide into my skin like butter. This was magical thinking. The fishhook needle bore into my skin with a vengeance. We nodded off, puked, ate cookies, and nodded some more. He wandered back to the bar at some point. He came back the next day smelling like cheap vodka and sweat to do it all over again. Now, a few days later, I am broke.

Ah, of course—the number in my wallet. It starts to come back to me. This guy wants me to call him as soon as I get paid again. I owe him $20 for a shitty bag of coke that I split with my friends, plus I think I might have let him feel my tits at the bar to get him to buy me a few drinks. My life is a constant series of new highs and mostly lows. I take inventory: several bags of heroin, cocaine, a few Vicodin, and cheap booze. *I had a productive weekend*, I think, as I sit here feeling my loneliness.

I haven't had my phone turned on at this apartment, or else my mother would surely be calling by now. The last time I saw her, she knew something was going on with me. It's been a few months since then. I had gotten a DUI trying to navigate my way back to West Chester under the influence of a few too many cocktails. For me to be able to continue in school, I had to move out of my parents' house in the suburbs and back closer to downtown Cincinnati. At least when I lived with my parents there were some constraints on my behavior. Now there were none. I imagined the next time I would see her. She would have to get my brother or someone to drive her to come get me to take me back to the house. We would do these check-ins once a month or so since the first D had come home on my report card. My mother was none too happy with what she saw as another rebellious phase. Between the black clothes and my new tattoo, my mother was wondering if I had suddenly become possessed by some kind of devil.

"Why haven't you called me?" she will inevitably ask.

During my last visit, my time was spent dodging eye contact. The sunglasses concealed the dark circles under my eyes. A long-sleeved shirt hid the bruise the syringe had made on my forearm. I had lost a few pounds, but nothing drastic enough to draw much attention. She wasn't focused on my appearance; for my mother, it is more about my mood. She's always interested in how I answer questions. As I sat in the living room sipping my diet soda that day, my mind formulated a million excuses.

My mom gets this look on her face when she is worried. She wears a shade of makeup that is slightly too dark and slightly too thick in a ring around her face. When she gets upset, the makeup crinkles by the corners of her eyes. I have seen this look many times. That day was the first time it was ever directed at me. Twenty years old is pretty late in life to start fucking up. I am making up for lost time. She never saw this coming. My progression from bookworm to party girl has thrown her off guard.

I had always been the "good girl." I was the child who had never given my parents any problems. For me, that meant I was invisible to them. My mother focused on my father, my father focused on drinking, and I focused my attention on anything that would get my mind off my misery. Books were my first fix, even before food. I could read a book a day. I could spend hours and hours sitting in my room, absorbed in the stories of other people. I liked to imagine myself as part of the story. I could forget myself as I turned those pages. It was hard for me to live in my own skin. My parents saw me as well-behaved and studious. The reality was I was extremely depressed. I didn't know a name for it, but I knew this feeling of darkness that would overwhelm me. I would lie around watching television for days at a time trying to escape my surroundings. Inside, I felt as if I wanted to scream at the top of my lungs. Or break things if I could muster the energy. I remember the feeling of wanting to disappear, which as a teen became a feeling of wanting to die. It was only in hindsight that my mother realized I'd been having trouble finding ways to cope. I kept things bottled up for so many years that I was bound to implode or explode. I chose the former. Everything feels like it is crashing around me.

During that last visit, I had stuffed my face with the food she brought to me. I hadn't had a solid meal in days.

"Tracey . . . I am asking you a question," she said.

I tried to put her off by telling her, "I have just been busy, Mom. I have school and work."

This was half true and half lie. I did go to work. I needed that money. School was a different story. I had been to five classes since the semester started.

She tried to get me to look at her. I didn't want anyone to see me, least of all her.

"You know how I worry," she told me. *Yes. I know*, I thought to myself.

In fact, I have started to worry about myself. I occasionally hear a faint voice in the back of my mind asking me what the hell I am doing. I suppose it is what is left of my conscience. I drown that voice at happy hour. *Let me live my life*, I tell it. I spent so many years as a depressed fat girl, this is my time to enjoy life. I almost believe my own lies. Almost. There are moments of sobriety interlaced with the intoxication that creates humiliation. I need more and more substances to cover up the mess I have made of my life.

My mother loves to talk on the phone on Sundays. My visits have become fewer and farther between, so she depends on those phone calls. Sunday is our day for connection. For a few moments, we can be a normal mother and daughter again. For as long as I can remember, Sunday always has been a special day to us. No matter how much my father drank during the week, he usually made an attempt to be sober on

Sunday. He would get stuff done around the house, almost as if we were a normal family. He would go out on the lawn mower or do the grocery shopping. My mom would look out the window, setting her hair for the week, while he raked up the leaves. She wore a modified beehive long after it went out of style. She could only sleep on her back for fear any other position would destroy her look. She coated her hair in White Rain hairspray, sipping on her Maxwell House coffee in her frosted green mug. My father worked as an engineer, sixty- to eighty-hour workweeks with lots of travel. He was rarely home. When he was, it frequently would spiral into chaos. Mostly I was raised by my mother. She went back to work temporarily when I was six and never left. She worked as an executive secretary during a time when secretaries were known as "girls." My parents work hard. If they ever find out what I am doing, I will be one big fucking disappointment.

My mind is going a million miles a minute. That is one of the drawbacks of cocaine. It makes me think too much. I put my hands across my eyes. Both are throbbing in unison. I am going to go back to sleep and pray for better luck.

Six months later, I decide it is time for me to get away from Cincinnati. "Decide" might not be the right word. My terrible choice in company has made the decision for me. My mom used to tell me, "Show me who your friends are and that will tell me who you are." Well, my friends are slowly becoming people I would have called cutthroats and junkies. I guess I am becoming one as well. I thought I was so different from all the other users. I was a person who cared. I would take people in for a few days here and there, people off the street who were traveling through the city following the Grateful Dead or some punk rock band. They would tell me their stories of dope sickness or some other drug-related malady that I thought was surely in their head. *How could some little pill or powder have such a huge hold on you?* I thought to myself as I dismissed their complaints as fiction. I was somehow above them because I was too strong to get hooked on anything. I had gone all these years without any issues. It was easy to delude myself into believing I must be fine. The evidence was stacking up against me, yet I turned the cloudiest of blind eyes.

My judgment has gotten as low as my standards. One blurry night recently changed the course of my life. I was hanging out at a bar—the way I would spend most of my evenings after work—with a friend of a friend, since my usual happy hour companion had passed out early at my place. We'd been downing some cheap fortified wine called Cisco. It's known on the street as "liquid crack" and tastes like grape lighter fluid. This man used to go out with one of my friends. We spent our time exchanging stories about her. She was a beautiful woman with long blonde hair. She wore liquid eyeliner and always had a Newport hanging out of one corner of her mouth. I loved her and he had loved her. We had this thing in common. Everything else was so very different. He had recently been released from prison. That should have scared me, but the liquor gave me artificial courage.

He was entertaining me with stories about the predicament he was in that was like something out of a gangster movie. He owed some money to a loan shark. *Do those really exist?* I thought as I sipped my gin and tonic. I tried to focus on pacing myself so I wouldn't throw up later. In the morning, he was planning to present the loan shark with the money: $2,240, to be exact. He had the cash with him, but he said he was a little short on his debt. I had seen the movies. "Are they going to break your legs?" I asked. He laughed at my ignorance. Not at what they would do to him, but at how I stupidly did not understand that these things really existed.

When we finally staggered back to my apartment, our noisy laughter woke my sleeping houseguest, who got up and left quickly. No time to swap stories with two drunk fools on a Thursday night. Unfortunately, the houseguest took something else with him. Without my knowledge, he clipped my drinking partner. My friend didn't notice that his money was gone until he woke up later, and our earlier laughter turned into terror.

"These people are going to kill me, Tracey," he told me frantically.

He flipped over my mattress in vain.

I offered naïvely, "Let me help you look for it."

He pushed me back down.

"No!" he told me. "You have done quite enough."

If I wasn't still so drunk, I would be more afraid.

"Seriously," I said. "Let me help."

Then I saw it. That look in his face. He picked up a pair of broken scissors and put them up against my face. A theft had turned into a hostage situation. I wasn't going anywhere, I wasn't doing anything, until he let me go. I instantly felt sober. He was angry and he was desperate. This made a person dangerous.

I would see that look again. I would see it in the face of a rapist, hopeless addicts, and abusive boyfriends. It was a look that I had never seen growing up in suburban Ohio. This look was one of terror. It was my face reflected in his eyes—I say "reflected" because when he looked at me, I saw nothing but a frenzied stare. No emotion but anger, all of it directed at me.

"If I don't find this money, I am going to kill you, bitch," he told me.

He pushed the scissors toward my face again.

"In fact, I am not going to kill you," he continued. He was so angry spit was starting to come out of his mouth.

"I am going to put your eyes out so you have to live the rest of your life this way." I believed him. In my gut I knew these were facts he was giving me, not idle threats.

As he tore apart every inch of my apartment, I sat frozen. He explained to me that these were the type of people who would not forgive him for not having the money. He dragged me around the city in the dark, fruitlessly trying to find my houseguest. It wasn't the fact that it was my houseguest who had stolen this man's money. What mattered to me was that he didn't believe me. When he finally decided to abandon me, I formulated an idea about how to get enough money to escape the city. It would take a few days. I would have my college tuition check refunded to me. It was break time between quarters. It would take a while before my parents would realize what had happened. I had to find some way to fix the situation. More importantly, I had to find a way to get out of his reach—NOW. There was once a time when I was innocent, when I believed the world was a good place full of good people. That time was over.

Within a few days, I was on a Greyhound with $900 and no idea what I was going to do with myself. I just knew that I had to get away from immediate danger.

In my mind, there were two junkie choices: New York and San Francisco. If I was going to take a "vacation," I certainly wanted it to involve drugs. The incident in my apartment had me looking over my shoulder in fear for my life. I needed an escape. I needed it now. I certainly intended to return when things calmed down. How long would it take this person to realize I didn't take his money? If I was going to hide out for a few weeks, I figured I might as well enjoy my time. Hell, I thought, I might even be able to bring back a few bags and double my money. People I knew did this all the time. I could get back the $900 and go back to school. The plan was slowly taking shape. I knew people in both SF and NYC, places I was *sure* I could get heroin. New York didn't seem that appealing. I had been there in 1988 with a few friends. We had slept in our car at Tompkins Square Park. We drank blackberry-flavored brandy to stay warm in the cold city air. That was the first time I saw a dead person on the street. His body was blocking my path. I asked my friend, "What do I do?" He said, "This is New York, step over him." We had gotten loaded on something or other, but I never got the hang of navigating the dope spots. I decided I would try my hand at San Francisco. The warm California sun would do wonders for my mood while I worked to straighten out my life back in Cincinnati.

I contacted a friend from high school. He was attending the University of San Francisco. He agreed to let me stay in his dorm for a few days. Unfortunately for that relationship,

I was a train wreck from day one. All I could think was, *Where can I get some drugs?* I was on a mission, as I called it. I knew that if I could find Jeremy, I would be able to get high. I had heard he had advanced to harder drugs. Plus, I trusted him. Either way, I had to find something. My money was burning a hole through my pocket.

Up until this point, I had used drugs but never had easy access to them. The seasoned junkies I met out at the bars who were traveling through the city used to snicker at me. They told me I was the "kind of person that had a job." I wasn't a hustler. I would learn later I was the type of person who was known as a "mark," because I was completely naïve about the ways of the drug world. In Ohio, I went to school or worked or both. San Francisco would become a total departure from everything I knew of life. When I left my hometown, I cut myself off from my support system, both emotionally and financially. No longer could I turn to trusted friends or my parents. I had to find my own way as I waded waist-high through the gutter of human garbage. It became perfectly normal to have no job and no place to live, and to use drugs outside.

When I was a teenager, I used to listen to the band Fang. They would sing songs about the Tenderloin district in San Francisco. Those songs spoke to me. They made me feel as if being a junkie was the ultimate act of rebellion. Everything I had hated about my life was in the lyrics. The isolation, the depression, and the feeling of not belonging anywhere in society. I had seen both my parents work hard their entire lives to obtain financial gains, yet they never seemed happy. Maybe the solution to happiness came with not caring what others thought about me. It sounded like everything I wanted from life. I wanted that feeling of complete freedom and not giving a fuck about anything. I had always worried about my weight, my grades, and my parents, why other kids tormented me. My life had been filled with so many *expectations*. Be a good girl. Get good grades. Ignore the fact that my father is drunk. Don't tell anyone what goes on in this house. Keep everything inside. Smile—what do you have to cry about? I was reminded that I had everything—everything—except I wanted to kill myself and I didn't know why. My ex-boyfriend had told me I was worthless. Maybe he was right. For now, I wanted to be relieved of my burdens.

On the way to my friend's dorm from the Greyhound station, the cab driver pointed out the window: "This is the Tenderloin. Do *not* come here." That moment will always be cemented in my memory. That was the day when I found everything I thought I wanted in one place. I had a return-trip ticket to Cincinnati in my bag. But I never made it back. My life was now in San Francisco.

I stepped onto the bus that very first night after dropping off my things at my friend's dorm. "Can you tell me which bus will take me downtown?" I asked the driver. "I need the Tenderloin."

I felt instantly overstimulated by the insanity of my new environment. It was complete chaos. In Ohio I had never seen people use drugs out in the open, with the few exceptions being when I stole quick glances from the bus while going past the housing projects. In the Tenderloin, drugs were everywhere. There was crack on one street, people high on meth on another. There were hookers walking the streets in the middle of the day—men, women, trans folk, and many who looked well under the age of consent. I was in awe of the fact that I could buy needles on the street corners for $2. There was even a place I could exchange them for clean ones, a program that was completely absent in Ohio. People slept anywhere and everywhere on the street. AIDS was in full swing. I had never met anyone with the virus in Cincinnati. Now, it seemed as if the signs and faces of the epidemic were everywhere. It seemed like everyone had a cane or an oxygen tank. I was smart enough to be afraid and naïve enough to push forward anyway.

Within days, I was full of so many different kinds of drugs. I didn't find Jeremy right away, but I found ten other people just like him. Eager young men in need of money and a chick to hang out with them. Within a few days my friend asked me politely to leave. I certainly didn't blame him. The second night I was in the city, I was returned to his room by strangers. I had passed out in the center of town. I was slumped against a stop sign when some Good Samaritans graciously offered to transport me back to the dorms. "Where do you live?" they asked. "Ohio" was my reply. A new acquaintance thought he was helping me out when he gave me a Klonopin mixed with some other kind of medication to chase the heroin. I had $800 tucked in my sweaty bra.

In the first month I was in the city, I found the heroin, Xanax, crystal methamphetamine, cheap alcohol, and crack cocaine. It did not take long to burn through what money I had on drugs and hotel rooms. When I had brief moments of consciousness, I would think about my mother.

I knew she would be expecting her Sunday phone call. But I could not pick up the phone. I was too ashamed. The truth was too hard to explain. I had abandoned school to live on the streets of a strange city. But I had no shortage of excuses. She would be better off without me. It was painful for me to think of how I must be hurting her. I couldn't bear to hear her voice. She would never understand. How could she? I barely understood myself. I eventually called anyway. At first I told her I was on vacation. Then I said I was looking into a new school. At some point along the way, I simply stopped calling. She had to find out from my landlord that I was not coming home. I thought it might be better for everyone involved if I just disappeared. I did—I disappeared into a chemical coma. I felt brief moments of happiness. Most of all, I felt numb. That was what I thought I needed.

I made friends quickly, other kids who had left their homes to escape to the city. Many of them were fleeing abusive parents. Some of them had come out as gay, lesbian, or transgender, only to be kicked out into the streets. We would huddle together on Market Street sharing beers while swapping stories about the places we wanted to see across the U.S. Every week, it seemed like there was a new group of people. It was easy at first, sleeping in little groups on the street or in abandoned buildings. The money for hotels was long gone. For $20, I could pull together enough drugs or alcohol to satisfy my tiny habit. But that honeymoon phase didn't last long. The romance of being on the road soured as my habit increased. I had never been exposed to heroin long enough to know how quickly it takes hold of a person.

It was as if one day I woke up with an unquenchable thirst, and the only thing that satisfied me was that drug.

I had to find ways to support a growing habit.

I ran into Jeremy one afternoon when I was sick with the beginning of a withdrawal. He told me he would fix me up at "his" apartment. I don't know why I actually believed for a second that it was his. He was living with a blue-haired stripper. She was taking care of all the bills while he made a few dollars here and there facilitating minor drug deals. He seemed genuinely happy to see me, though troubled.

As he cooked up the drugs, he nearly burned a hole in his leather pants. He looked like he had stepped out of London in the late '70s with his perfect English punk attire. He seemed slightly out of place on that hot day. He didn't have a shirt on, and I could see the scars from where he had been cutting himself again.

"Why are you here?" he asked me.

Because . . . I didn't know anymore.

I held my syringe in my hand as he did his issue. He had given me a clean one, a new one in fact. I was embarrassed to admit I didn't know how to inject myself. Over a year of IV use and I still hadn't learned. It had never been hard to find someone to inject me, as long as I was willing to share. I had always been afraid of needles (once when I needed a vaccination it had taken five medical staff people to hold down my hysterical body). Now here I was, blindly holding out my arm to be injected with this strange drug known as black tar heroin.

He turned to me as the drugs hit him. He could see I needed him to inject me. This was such a strange scene. I thought I had tried to save him once. Now he was helping me. He had everything while I was out on the street.

"You can't hit yourself?" he said. He shook his head in disbelief as he grabbed a shoelace to wrap around my arm.

"Get out," he told me. "Get out of this city. Go back home. Forget this place."

I laughed to myself. What did he know? He had been here only a few months longer than I had. Everything had seemed fine so far. I felt like I was on an extended vacation.

The great adventure came to a screeching halt when I realized soon after that I was strung out. For years before that, I had truly believed that being strung out was all psychological. I remember remarking on how weak-minded someone must be to get dependent on some little substance. It is different when you are the one who is strung out. I got to experience that pain firsthand. This wasn't just the "junkie flu." This was an all-encompassing feeling that took over my body, my mind, and my soul. We used to have a saying: "Are you dedicated to the cause?" Except this wasn't religion or politics—this was something far more serious. You could separate the casual user from what we called a "dope fiend" by the things one was willing to do to get money for drugs. When I became strung out, I was dedicated to the cause. I was willing to go to any length to keep from feeling that terrible sensation that came with withdrawal. The twitching legs, the snot dripping from my nose, the feeling of desperation. Heroin became the love of my life. I would do anything to be together just one more time.

"Fuck, I'm getting sick," one of my new friends told me.

She was a young woman who had just left her house in Marin. She told me she was twenty-one, but I suspected she was younger. Eighteen? Nineteen? I found out later she was just out of high school. She had started mixing with the "wrong crowd" during her senior year. We were thrown together through a mixture of poor choices and desperation. I had been educated by a few more seasoned female users while we sat around and waited for the dope man. They would explain that a young woman alone in the city was not safe if she chose to use drugs. One of a few things would happen. She would overdose, only to be put out on the sidewalk. She would end up stripping. She would be supporting not just her own habit but also that of her "musician" boyfriend. He'd call himself a musician—all his equipment went to the pawn shop long, long ago. Finally, a young woman might get "turned out" by a pimp to prostitution. Men see women as dollar signs. There is an untapped gold mine in her pants. Everyone wants a piece of women like us. Those more experienced women learned the hard way; they were trying to impart their wisdom. I listened to the best of my ability. I got with my new friend so we could pool our money, but now this relationship was about to come to an end.

She was complaining about being sick. I hated to see her like this. As much as I didn't want to admit it, I had developed some feelings for her. I had a crush on this girl. She liked me, too. I could never be myself in Ohio; my being attracted to women would have been too much for my conservative community. Our relationship wasn't based on sex—it was emotional in nature. This was the first time I had felt as if someone liked me for more than just what I had in my pants. She made me feel like I was okay just the way I was. She liked to read books to me and tell me her deepest secrets. She told me she left because her stepfather had been molesting her since she was thirteen. She finally got up the courage to leave the house after her mother refused to believe her. I admired her strength. A boyfriend got her started on drugs, then left her for better opportunities. She had no street smarts, no experience. In reality, neither did I. I was just a few months ahead of her in this life.

I started to think of things we could do for money.

"Well, let's go up to Larkin and O'Farrell," I suggested.

Larkin and O'Farrell is an intersection near a center that helps homeless youth, which means that corner attracts a special type of predator, the type looking for young women. I had been stopped there many times by men looking for sex. Before we could even agree on an amount, they always wanted to know my age. Apparently I looked sixteen, because I walked away with cash a few times.

I never thought I would have sex with anyone for money. Heroin made it so easy. It asked me how this was any different from the random hookups in bars I used to have. This time, it told me, I could get paid for it. My newfound friends agreed. Junkies on the street had the perfect guy for me that first time. He was safe. He told me I was a goddess. The next time was easier. I was stupid to sell myself short. No one had really wanted me all my life. Now men nearly ran their cars off the road to spend time with me. It seemed to make sense. I was a feminist. It was my body, my choice. I was unable to see that the drugs were making all the choices for me.

I continued. "Maybe we can catch one of those kids with money going to the youth center. If not, we can do a quick date and meet back here."

Her silence told me everything.

"No." She shook her head at me.

Here was the difference between a casual user and where I was in life. She was willing to sit around in withdrawal until easy money or drugs came her way. She didn't understand. I didn't want her to. Part of me was wishing I could be like her. Two cute young women could sometimes get gifts from strangers—seemingly with no expectations for sex in return. In reality there was a "system" with the unspoken rule that all debts would eventually be collected. No one around here got anything for free. We all paid one way or another. But my heroin habit was pushing me past the point of waiting for a free gift to come along. The eight-hundred-pound gorilla on my back needed to be fed.

I started to raise my voice. "While you are willing to scrounge money for drugs, looking for change in a couch to support a $5 habit, I need some REAL money. I am supporting a $30- to $50-a-day habit." She could not understand the things I was willing to do. I was glad she couldn't. Maybe she wouldn't end up like me.

The party ended for me when I traded my stability for my next fix.

I tried to explain to her, "If you aren't making money, you are walking around sick. No one is helping you. It is just us."

She shook her head at me again.

One of the older junkies had told me early on, "You better be shoplifting, selling your ass, or working the hell out of anyone that crosses your path. Or all of these things. You are getting your teeth pulled for pain meds to sell. You are living on the street. You are alone in the world."

My girl was not willing to do any of these things. I was proud of her for this. I envied her ability to say no, but I knew this would be the end of our friendship. A few days later, I put her on the bus to stay with a relative in Michigan. She made it out alive. Years later, she sent me letters thanking me for taking care of her. I cried when I saw them. She had contacted my mother for my address.

"Who is this person?" my mother asked me.

"A friend," I told her.

What else could I say? I wasn't even sure myself what the relationship had been.

Once I had put her on the bus, there was nothing left in my way. *I need to clean my ass up*, I thought. I need to get a place, a base of operations. Everything good is gone. The dates don't like me all dirty. And I'm 100 percent dedicated to the cause. I started using to forget this pain. Now this life was all just fucking painful. I was not the same woman who left Ohio. For the first time in my life, I was strung out and alone.

Chapter 3

CLEAN AND SOBER SUCKS

Black tar heroin—a dark, sticky substance that's dirtier than the white powder version—is well-known for destroying its host. There was no symbiotic relationship between it and me. My body was ravaged by the very substance that maintained my existence. By twenty-seven years old, I was far from the wide-eyed young woman who had stepped off the bus from Ohio. I was a hardened soul with years of jails, homelessness, and a few abusive relationships under my belt. The only thing I had to be proud of was that I was able to survive in a world that killed so many. I became the things that had once made me so afraid.

I was unpredictable. I was occasionally violent. Most of all, I had a tenuous hold on sanity. I had spent time locked in a psychiatric facility for three days on an involuntary hold. I had to admit those were some of my best days in recent years—I was safe, well fed, and able to rest without fear of being assaulted.

My life as an IV drug user had hit a low point. I had run out of veins, leaving me little choice but to stick syringes in the soles of my feet. When users run out of "surface" veins, there are a few alternatives. One is using the jugular vein, the one located in your neck. This can be very dangerous since it is located so close to your brain. I knew someone who died from a blood clot a few days after choosing this path. The second choice is using the femoral, or the vein in the groin. This one cannot be seen. There is also a high risk of breaking off the needle, as I had seen happen to my former lover. A third option is called "muscling," or shooting the drugs directly into the muscle. This has caused many a soft tissue infection, also known as an abscess. The last and certainly least attractive choice was to quit using altogether. By this time, using felt like knitting needles were tearing away at my skin. I was barely able to walk a few yards at a time, yet I continued to trek up and down the city streets for a few hours a day to sell heroin to junkies like myself before coming home to my hotel in the Tenderloin district.

The Hotel Kinney was known as a "trap house" because it was filled with junkies and small-time dealers, and people would get trapped there. Young women stepped off the Greyhound from the suburbs, as I did, and never left. I paid $35 a night to live with roaches, rodents, and a mix of immigrants who were trying to start a new life and junkies who stood a good chance of ending theirs in one of the empty rooms. But this particular night I wasn't thinking about my neighbors as I dragged my tired ass up the stairs. I just needed to keep putting one swollen foot in front of the other.

I had gone up almost a full flight of stairs when I heard the front door open behind me. Half turning, I saw two cops coming into my building. I knew they were looking for me before I even heard them say my name to the front desk clerk.

One cop spied me on the stairs. "You there," he called out. "Stop." I froze, trying not to panic. *Stay cool, for fuck's sake*, I told myself. I couldn't make a run for it even if I wanted to. They asked me for directions to Tracey's room. I told them I didn't know who they were talking about. I later learned the police had only my name and a vague description of what I looked like from a confidential informant.

I let them pass me before turning around and, trying not to appear too freaked, went back downstairs to a small pocket underneath the stairwell. I didn't need much room. Starved by daily drug use, I was a walking skeleton. Underneath my three T-shirts you could see all my ribs. I pushed my body into the crawlspace.

As I crouched in the enveloping dust, trying not to cough, a rat ran past me. Until then, I hadn't realized that rats could run upstairs. I heard the scraping of its claws traversing the steps and was struck by the realization that this creature was free to roam while I was stuck in this hole. I was on a downward spiral. For the first time in years, I didn't have a boyfriend. The latest one, despite being an addict himself, had found me to be too much work.

He left me with a cocaine habit on top of my heroin one. I would get powder cocaine as a bonus from my dealer if I produced the correct amount of money for my packages of heroin. I had no one to blame but myself. I had refused rehab two years earlier despite the urgings of my parents. They had arranged for me to be transported from San Francisco to a center near my hometown. They became particularly concerned after I'd gone to the hospital to have a procedure to drain an abscess on my arm. This was in addition to infections I already had brewing on three other limbs. When I woke up from surgery in handcuffs, for a few seconds I considered going to rehab in Ohio. Yet despite all the evidence that it was time to stop, I was just not ready. I didn't want to waste their money.

This time, crouched under the stairs two years later, I finally felt it—it was time to stop. This time would be different. There were no more worthwhile highs, there was no more joy in drugs for me. I was not living anymore, just carving out a dull existence in my bruised flesh. I was done.

I waited until the cops left—they never found my room. I paid by the night so I moved rooms every few days. I made up my mind as I untangled my body from the hiding place, brushing dust and bits of cobwebs from my hair. I'd evaded them this time, but whenever the police found me, I decided, I would go willingly and try to get clean.

Many addicts find their way to recovery by accident. Mine was more of a planned surrender. When I got to my room, I packed a suitcase and put it in the closet, hoping I'd be able to take it with me when I was arrested. As soon as people saw you leave the hotel in handcuffs it was like an invitation to come into your space and steal your stuff. Every time I got arrested, I would come home to find nothing left. When I got out of jail this time, I didn't want to start over with nothing.

The police came to my door just after midnight a few days later. My best friend Mike was crashed out on my bed after we had been drinking some beers. Mike was the first person I had known who had been an addict and gotten clean. Unfortunately, he did not stay that way. We used to sit up sometimes on our sleeping bags in the cold alleys of San Francisco before the sun came up as we shed a few tears over the slow deterioration of our lives. Mike did not do heroin, but as an addict he understood me. He was always the first person to defend me. No matter what happened, it seemed as if Mike was there to help me pick up the shattered pieces. Once a man who had assaulted me walked into our den to score drugs. He didn't realize he was walking into my space, my rules. Mike jumped from the couch. "Is this the guy?" he said.

"Yes." It was him. How could I miss the face?

"Did you jack off on this girl?" Mike demanded.

"I don't know," the man said.

"How the fuck do you not know?" Mike said, then turning to me, he said, "Beat the shit out of him, Tracey." I froze. I couldn't do it. The man seemed so harmless and small without his knife, but I was still afraid of him. Just letting him go was not an option for Mike. It went against the law of the street. Mike beat him up for me.

Mike and I would drink St. Ides, listen to Geto Boys, and talk about getting clean in between binges. He even helped me kick a few times. He would bring me water while I twitched and flopped on his couch for four days, only to see me go back again and again. As I would return to heroin over and over again, I saw his faith in me dwindle. Even among drug users, there is stigma attached to heroin use. An IV heroin user is the lowest of the low. Those who smoke or snort heroin have some superior standing, because it is believed among non-users and users alike that they are somehow not as addicted as those who inject. As a meth user, Mike was confused as to why I returned to something that caused me so much trouble, Stimulants create the illusion that there is no dependency. "I am just using this because I want to . . . I can quit when I want," Mike told me. Apparently he "wanted" to use it all day every day for months at a time. Heroin was much less subtle. Every morning the call of the sickness would abuse me. *Bitch, get up!* it told me. There was no reprieve. I never had a pimp. I never needed one. Heroin was pimping me, getting me to do whatever was necessary to make money to feed my habit. This was something Mike could not understand.

When he came over that night, I gave him a big hug. He had heard I was dealing now and wanted to see the damage. To celebrate, I plied him with weed and alcohol. I knew he would be too tired to leave. He didn't realize I had already had a celebration of my own with crack on top of heroin on top of speed. I suspect he was used to it by now. He had become accustomed to my need to be high every second of every moment to make it through the day. I was so high that I accidentally opened the door to the police right away when I heard the knock. With one turn of the knob, I turned my future.

As soon as I saw the police, I immediately put my hands up and said, "All the dope is mine," so they would let Mike go. It only took a minute for them to find the heroin. I had picked up my normal package from my dealer, thirty balloons. I had injected three. The remainders were strewn on the bed. Normally I carried them around in a condom stuffed into my vagina. When I started using my body as a carrying case, all the romance of using was officially dead for me. I was fucked-up beyond reason on those three bags, but like the honor student I once was, I did some quick math. There was still a half ounce left. Shit.

As I felt the tightness of the cold steel handcuffs, I started to ask the cops to get the suitcase out of the closet, but then I stopped myself. Did I really want to return to this? Fuck it. I decided to leave everything, walking out with only the pajamas and the pair of shoes I was wearing. I was unsure about the future, but I knew this: I did not want to come back to the room, the Tenderloin, or the life. I told myself this would be the last time I would take this walk of shame to the police car. I gave the Hotel Kinney one last glance through the haze of my sedation. Little did I know I would be back, living around the corner, six months later. Surprisingly, I would return clean.

I did not know what awaited me in "recovery." I had not known anyone who had gotten off drugs and stayed off. All I knew was that if I didn't make the most of this opportunity, the next time I would get pulled out of this hotel, I would be on the way to the morgue.

Like many addicts, I started my recovery in handcuffs. After a series of questions about my medical history, I was allowed to drag a mattress onto the cold floor of what is called the "kick tank." The cell contained no bunks and was filled with addicts in various states of sickness curled up on the floor. I had been to jail many times, but I had never been deemed enough of a junkie to be sent here. I had heard stories over the years of people dying in here. I knew pain awaited me.

My cold-turkey detox started twelve hours later, after the drugs started to leave my body, in a four-person cell. On the first day I was still feeling the effects of the drugs; they started to leave my body on the second day, along with what seemed like all my fluids. We were each given a plastic bag to hold our vomit. I had teary eyes, vomiting, and diarrhea all at the same time, while my legs twitched with involuntary muscle spasms, hence the term "kicking." The jail provided some over-the-counter medications like Tylenol and Doan's Pills. We had to provide evidence we had puked to get a shot of Compazine, an antinausea drug normally given to schizophrenics. Only alcoholics got Librium to help control their fear and anxiety. The reality was everyone needed it. We were all going out of our minds.

At the end of day two, I was shaking so hard and it was so noisy in the jail, I felt like I had boarded a rocket ship. Destination: Unknown. My body was detoxing from who knows how many substances. I was hallucinating so badly I started searching for syringes in my blanket because instinct told me drugs were the only thing that could keep me from dying.

The day you stop using is the day your recovery starts. Recovery begins with the body and slowly works on the mind. The body shakes and shivers as layers of toxic substances are cleared away to make room for something new. It is as if you are shedding your skin. The body must be cleared of the very thing it desires. The body wants to pace, wants to run away. You feel like your heart is going to beat out of your chest and then you realize you cannot get out of bed.

By the third day my mind was clear enough to question everything. Recovery is both a noun and a verb. I did not know who I was any more than I knew what to do next. I got into a fight with another inmate, about something. She lunged at me, thinking she would take advantage of my vulnerable state. At that moment, I was in need of an outlet and she was it. As she jumped on top of me, I reached for her neck, pulling her off me with all my nervous energy. As I brought my other arm back to beat the hell out of her I had a moment of clarity. I am done fighting. I am not doing this anymore. *When I get out of this motherfucking kick tank,* I thought, *I am asking to go to a program.* Fuck this life.

This was my eleventh time kicking heroin, and it would be my last.

Dressed in orange pants, orange sweatshirt, orange T-shirt, orange socks, and even orange panties, I appeared in court a month or so later. I was on a no-bail hold for violation of my probation. My only deviation from the standard uniform worn by the other prisoners was a piece of glove that I had torn and used to tie my slicked-back hair into a ponytail, which I hoped made me look more respectable, appealing, and worthy of a break.

"Ms. Helton, do you understand and agree to this sentence?"

I nodded. "Yes, Your Honor." This was the only time I spoke.

The prosecuting attorney stood up, and all I heard was, "I object." What the fuck. My probation officer had recommended that I get a nine-month sentence that included a drug treatment program. With time for good behavior, I would be released in five months. This objection could destroy my chances of going to rehab at all.

I'm sure the prosecutor looked at a piece of paper and saw that I was a repeat offender who had been caught in possession of a half ounce of heroin. She probably thought she was doing society a favor by protecting it from someone like me. In reality, I was putting a good portion of those drugs up my own arm on a daily basis. My life had been reduced to finding fulfillment wrapped in plastic bags. Now this—going to a program—was all I had left to live for. *Bitch, sit down!* All the poor decisions I had ever made in my life flashed before my eyes before the judge shut her down.

He agreed to send me to treatment instead of prison. If I did not complete the program, I would automatically be sentenced to three and a half years in state prison. It was a risk, but one I was willing to take. I finally started to breathe. I had never left jail and stayed clean. In fact, I had never stayed clean while in jail. The cravings had always overtaken my desire to try something different. A person in the know like myself would have access to a wide array of substances even behind bars. I had requested to be put in the "treatment" section of the jail this time. I was finally committed to something besides getting high. As the judge pointed out, this was "the first intelligent decision" I had made in a decade.

I was put into a residential treatment program for criminal offenders, meaning we all came from jail or prison. This made the place both sexually charged and dangerous. There were roughly ten men for every female in the facility. When I got off the bus from jail, a pack of men were waiting to greet us. I felt like a bloody steak in front of a bunch of lions looking for their next meal. I learned later that on smoke breaks the men would place bets on who was going to have sex with which of the incoming females.

When women walk into rehab they find the same type of men, if not the very same man, they are trying to escape, making it truly difficult for them to reset their lives. It didn't take long before many of my peers were having quickies in stairwells or on the Dumpster behind the building. Those twelve-step meetings ended in a few pregnancies.

Whenever I had imagined rehab before I got there, I suppose I thought of it as some sort of well-lit health spa, with time to relax to ease back into society. The treatment facility was the exact opposite of what I had expected. In fact, the place was just one step up from jail. It was in a large brick former warehouse with beds on three floors. Women were placed on the first floors where there were twenty bunks in two rooms. The beds were never full. Many women I met felt pressured by family responsibilities to immediately return home. Time and time again, I would see a woman crying on a pay phone in the hall and see her bed empty the next day. The women tended to fight on a daily basis— anything to distract them from the knowledge that their children were sitting in foster care while they were watching TV in the women's lounge. The stories I heard there made me uncomfortable. They were *The Jerry Springer Show* crossed with the worst horror movie, except these stories were real. As if on cue, the women would sit in a circle and tell stories of the children they had lost, their rapes, or years of molestation at the hands of someone they had trusted. I felt the impact of their stories, but I couldn't make the tears flow, not even for myself.

On the Sunday after I arrived, everyone was required to be in the "house" for a group meeting. I was excited to see everyone at one time. Eighty of us crammed ourselves into the cafeteria, each with his or her own story. Some used crack, others meth; some were alcoholics on parole for their fourth DUI. A few had jobs and children, and there were those who were there just to get off "paperwork."

The man who facilitated the meeting was well dressed, with a gold chain around his neck and sunglasses on his head. He drove an old Porsche and sported new braces, paid for with his brand new dental insurance. He spoke about having one year clean, which seemed impossible to me.

A hush fell as he said, "Look around the room. To your right and left." He paused for effect. "Of everyone here, only two of you are going to make it."

Under the fluorescent lights, I felt people all around me lose confidence. Each of us was wondering, *How am I ever going to make it?* Instead of uplifting broken people, the pep talk planted the seed of doubt. It turned out the facilitator himself did not make it. A few years later, he died of a crack-induced heart attack.

I knew I would have to fight to keep from becoming a statistic. I later learned that in rehab made-up statements about recovery were often passed off as facts. More than once I heard people throw around the "statistic" that only 1 percent of heroin addicts get clean and stay clean. This was not very comforting to a person trying to stay clean. On top of that, my options were limited. If I failed to complete the program, I was going to prison for three and a half years. More than that, I was motivated by the fact that if I failed, I would die with a needle hanging out of my arm.

I told myself: *Of the eighty people in this room, seventy-nine will be fighting for that last spot, because I am going to be one who stayed clean.* Period. I was not returning to alleyways. I was not going back to pushing my belongings in a shopping cart. I was not returning to injecting myself ten times a day. In my mind, I almost felt lucky that I had hit such a low bottom. It made it that much easier to commit to a program. I was willing to try anything not to use drugs: meetings, groups, keeping a journal, talking about my feelings. I was tired and I was done with that life. DONE. I ran that car until the wheels fell off. Drugs held no more illusions for me.

In early recovery, life was an effort. One second I felt happy. The next I wanted to scream at someone for accidentally brushing against me. Then I would feel the need to apologize not only to that person but also to every single person I had ever wronged. I had no idea how to live. I felt like crying, but the tears did not come. I didn't feel like using. In fact, on many days I didn't feel anything at all. My life was gray and overcast.

What I needed was a distraction, and for that I went to the second and third floors, where the men lived. Walking down the hallway, I slowed down for a good look. After two and a half months in jail, I craved the presence of men, even if they brought out things I didn't like about myself. I admit my view of men was warped. For example, there was something so sweet about a man escorting you back to your apartment after you have taken too many drugs. He would get bonus points if he didn't press for sex. That to me was romance. But when a boyfriend brought me flowers, I threw them on the ground. "I wanted to do something special," one boyfriend had said. I was homeless at the time. What the fuck was I going to do with flowers? He should have brought me some tissues instead, since he had given me a bloody nose and a black eye.

On the way to breakfast one morning, I caught a man looking at me as I crossed the cafeteria. I quickly looked away but when I saw him later in the hallway, I didn't flinch. Women and men sat together at mealtimes on the third floor. The management there tried to make it a family atmosphere, but with the "brothers" trying to sleep with the "sisters," it was more like every man for himself.

When I finally earned enough trust for an afternoon away from the program, I quickly abused it. The man I had spotted and I both knew the rules: no sex between residents. Yet my first pass involved forty-five minutes in a hotel room with him. Never mind that he spoke almost no English and I spoke only halting Spanish. I had fooled myself into believing he cared for me. My first sober kiss since high school led to hurried sex. As I pulled my clothes from the floor, I saw the moment for what it was: two people using each other for an escape. When I returned to the treatment center, they were surprised to see me back so soon. With no explanation, I went to the women's floor and took a long shower. Instead of tamping down my feelings as I would normally do, I let my emotions flow as I put my head against the tiles, water running down the back of my neck, trying to wash away my regret.

Getting off drugs was just a small part of staying clean. After the chemicals left my body, I was flooded with a lifetime of memories I had tried to stuff down. Underneath my hard exterior was a person drowning in fear. Thinking about my childhood, I realized I had been hooked all along. I remembered getting my wisdom teeth pulled and the warm fuzzy bubble of the Vicodin I was given. I had vowed not to become an alcoholic like my father, but this seemed okay because a doctor had prescribed it. The Vicodin relieved me of the burden of my thoughts. Everything I needed was in one place. I did not need food, I did not need to worry, and I did not need anything but the feeling of the drug. I felt totally comfortable with the numbness. Life seemed like a breeze while I was on Vicodin. I was so naïve that I truly believed I could control any drug I took, unlike "weak" people. I quickly learned that drugs do not discriminate. They prey on your weakest instincts and insecurities, of which I had plenty.

Listening to the other people talk during "share" time at the rehab center, I realized much of what people said was lies and half-truths for the benefit of attracting the opposite sex. Being in the program was a lot like being back in high school. People would stand up to "confess" to the things they missed from their addiction—the apartment, women, money, fame—rather than the reasons they were really here. No one said, "I'm a loser," "I hate myself," or any of the things that were really in their heads. I felt as if no one there understood me, as if I was unique among addicts. In reality, I think I was leaving myself room for the chance of relapse by staying isolated. When Mike sent a message through one of the residents to meet him to play video games, I jumped at the chance. I needed a break. While I was in jail, I learned Mike had started using heavily again. But the last time I saw him I was being hauled away by the police. I wanted to reconnect.

As I walked up the hill to Mike's apartment, I heard a voice in my mind: *No.* I felt it as concretely as the hard bed I slept in each night. Was I really going to just sit there while he got high? Maybe I was developing a sense of right and wrong choices, because my inner compass pointed me in a different direction. Or maybe I was just scared. I tucked my tail between my legs and ran back to the center.

I called Mike that night from the pay phone in the hallway.

"I'm sorry," I told him.

He was pissed. "We can't hang out, Tracey."

"Maybe I can try to get away next week," I said halfheartedly.

"No, you won't," he said. "Because I am doing this and you are doing that."

He was right. I needed to stay on the sobriety path with no distractions. The question was whether I could stay the course. When I emerged from the program later, I would feel like an alien who had been dropped onto a different planet. Not only did I have no contact with the outside world for the ninety days of my court-ordered rehab, but I had lost years to my addiction. The world had moved on to email, pagers, and mobile phones while I still carried crumpled phone numbers and dimes for the phone booth.

I finally got up the nerve to call home after the foolish sex incident. I wanted my mother to believe that everything was going well in treatment. How could I explain that I had fucked up again? She would know something was wrong in my voice. I used the phone right outside the women's lounge. The receiver was stained with sweat and tears. In general, this phone only seemed to deliver bad advice and bad news from home. I was determined to reach my mother. I had called her from the holding cell the night I was arrested to tell her I was going to get into a program, and from that moment she had been my staunchest supporter. Unfortunately, this time my father answered the phone. This was the man who, when he was a teenager and the family horse died, was hooked up to the plow in its stead. This was the man who brought his prom date home to meet his parents, and she asked to use the bathroom, walked out, and never came back. I didn't expect my father to talk about his feelings on the phone, but I braced myself for the disappointment that I knew he must have felt. We had become estranged since I left Ohio, and I had rarely spoken to him in the past few years. I am sure he received progress reports from my mother. I had spent all those years judging him for his drinking. Now here I was, a twenty-eight-year-old heroin addict who had achieved nothing in life.

It wasn't so long before then that I had been telling him I wanted to apply to Princeton. I'd had stellar grades and started out my freshman year at the University of Cincinnati almost a year ahead of my peers. The admissions counselor had told me in my interview, "You're a one-of-a-kind student." Little did she know how true that would turn out to be.

On the phone, my dad characteristically did not provide me with comfort. Nevertheless, he told me what I needed to hear. "All your friends are in the cemetery or penitentiary," he said. I am sure he told me that because he loved me. He had some insight into my struggle.

If I faltered from this path, I knew I was headed for the grave. After I completed my time at the treatment facility, I moved to a transitional house. I wasn't ready to be released into the world completely raw. I didn't know if I ever would be. Recovery was not a soft pillow to land on after a hard fall. All I knew was that I wanted to be able to look at myself in the mirror. I wanted my body to be my own. I wanted to be free.

Chapter 4

WALK A DAY IN MY SHOES

I have no luck with shoes. That's what I was thinking as I stood in front of the ATM fiddling with the ankle strap of my left shoe. Between the permanent damage from shooting up in the soles of my feet and the extra weight I was now carrying, finding a decent pair was nearly impossible. I still had a mile left to walk home. Distracted by the expectation of my shoe turning into a slow torture device, I didn't notice the man approaching the ATM until I caught his round face out of the corner of my eye. He was close to six feet tall, well dressed and well groomed. He looked like a professional man. His eyes were an unusual color of gray with corners that crinkled as he smiled widely at me; his smile was one of recognition. I saw the flicker of his gold bracelet as he placed his hand on the wall close to me—too close—as if to engage me in a conversation.

Can't he see I'm using this damn machine? I concentrated on pushing the right buttons to take out money. Forty dollars to be exact. It will need to get me through the weekend. I felt him staring at me, and I turned my body to block my PIN number. *Some people are so rude*, I thought. What kind of asshole invaded the sacred space between a woman and her money machine?

He interrupted my irritation. "I see you really have changed," he said.

I quickly slipped the bills into my wallet and pretended I didn't hear him.

As I walked away, the images started to click: the man, the face, the voice, the bracelet. They were too familiar. My past, like the San Francisco fog I walked through on my way to work every morning, was murky yet inescapable. Where did this man fit? Was the memory a positive one or a deep regret I had buried inside myself to forget? I started on my mile-walk home, my irritation giving way to uneasiness and then shame with every step. I knew who this man was—how could I forget? He used to give me $40 if I would give him a blow job without using a condom. This was during the AIDS era, and I was adamant about using condoms with tricks. But a few times he convinced me to skip it with him. That day at the ATM I had taken out $40. The irony was not lost on me, or on him, I'm sure.

Home for me at this point was a single room in an old

hotel that had been converted into a sober living facility by the Salvation Army, where I could be required to submit to urinalysis at any time to prove I was clean. I had rolled up to the place one year ago, fresh from the treatment center, with two garbage bags of possessions that were either donated or paid for with my small income. For the first time in my life, I was attempting to be self-sufficient. My mother, of course, wanted to find some way to help me. My demonstrating that I was actually clean made her more determined to find ways to insert herself back into my life. She didn't need to give me anything in order to do that, though—I wanted her there. In that first year of recovery, I learned so much about my own dysfunctional relationships through the way she and I interacted. There was a fine line between providing someone with support and creating an unhealthy dependence. In feeling my way through recovery, I was trying to distinguish what that meant.

People discouraged me from moving back to the Tenderloin, but I had no choice—rents were lower there. Still, my rent was $360, which ate up almost all the money I earned at a call center doing phone surveys. I had found the job in the paper with the help of the rehab's job coach. I am not sure what the qualifications were to be the job coach, but there were rumors he was sleeping with male residents. The job paid $7 an hour. It was more than minimum wage and just enough to pay all my bills. It took twenty-nine years, but I was finally finding some independence.

I was surprised at how easy it was to get my job, even as a convicted felon. I was hired on the spot in my first interview. At first, my ego led me to believe I was so charming they just had to hire me. The reality was quite different. They simply needed bodies. The turnover rate became apparent as I watched people walk out in the middle of a shift on a daily basis. Well, I figured, the bar is so low that I can excel here. I reminded myself that I had convinced junkies to buy heroin from me despite the fact that I looked like an extra from Michael Jackson's *Thriller* video. Therefore, I must be capable of finding a way to get people to complete these surveys. I could be very convincing when I needed something. I turned that survival tactic into a workplace asset. In fact, it wasn't long before I was made a manager.

The other major benefit of the job was that it gave me enough downtime to work on learning my positive affirmations. I needed those, since I still felt as if my grip on my new life was precarious at best. The rehab center had sent me through a program designed specifically for criminal offenders. This week-long course showed me that I needed to learn to modify my behavior or I would end up back in jail or prison. When I completed the class, I was handed a set of four flashcards in a waterproof holder that fit in my pocket. *Fake it till you make it* was a catchphrase that chimed in my head. Okay, yes. I was willing to try it. I had flashcards with these phrases tucked away in my pocket (I was not yet confident enough in my femininity to carry a purse). I spent hours upon hours flipping through these cards between calls. I was hoping that changing the way I thought about myself would change the way I lived my life. I was back living in the Tenderloin; the steps of recovery needed to be inside me.

I enjoy my clean and sober lifestyle.
I enjoy being clean and sober.
I am a good person.
I wanted these things to be true.

My cravings for drugs were very sporadic, but they were still there. Since I had spent the bulk of my recovery in a controlled environment, I had gotten over that early phase of obsessing over drugs in a relatively safe place. But out on my own, my cravings would appear out of nowhere. They didn't come from what some might consider typical sources. The emotions that surfaced made for triggers I could not easily identify. Feelings were something that had always made me uncomfortable in my own skin, and they came up so unpredictably. Seeing people using drugs on the street did not give me cravings. Old places did not make me crave heroin either. I found that my triggers were more nuanced. The smell of vinegar, the scent of cheap coffee, or an alcohol smell could make my stomach flip in the same way it had when I was waiting for a hit. These are smells connected with the injection of cheap, adulterated tar heroin—the drug itself has a vinegary smell, coffee is often used to cut the dirtiest street-level version, and I would use alcohol pads to wipe up the blood that ran down my arms and legs after removing the needle. Living in this area was more of a bless- ing for me than a curse, though, because of the instant visual reminders of where I would return if I decided to use again.

I unlocked the deadbolt and stepped into my sparsely furnished room. It was nice that when I moved in it was semi-furnished. The guy who used to live there didn't bother to clean out the drawers of the only dresser. It contained his recovery books and journals. As soon as I got settled that first night out of treatment, I rocked back and forth on the bed. I was bugging out. I wanted to use so badly or at least go hang out in the usual spots that were just fifty feet outside my window, but I knew I would have ended up with a needle in my arm. How was I going to live? Like the addict I was, I ticked off my options: I could sell drugs and not use them. I could find a dealer to take care of me. I could find a trick and keep the money since now I was not on drugs. I was lonely and afraid of what I would do that night. I read in one of the recovery books left behind that "an addict alone is in bad company." I got out of my head and went to the nearest meeting, an atheist twelve-step meeting.

The meeting broke all the traditional twelve-step rules. It was perfect for me. People cross-talked, they spoke more than once, and there was more silence than I had experienced the entire time I was in residential treatment. I learned that night that it wasn't necessary to fill up a silence with words. Sometimes, the best response to a problem is to reflect on it in silence. I did not need to have an answer for everything. There was a young man there who talked about being four years clean. He was in his early twenties and beautiful to me. Not just because of his physical features, but because he was kind to me in ways I had not experienced from a man in years. After the meeting, he asked me if I wanted him to wait with me at the bus stop. When I waved goodbye to him that night, I knew that at least for that day I was not going to use. It broke my heart when he relapsed a few months later. Then I was told by the meeting leader that he had killed himself in his mother's house. In my moment of grief, I had resolved yet again that this would not be me.

A year later, here I was rubbing my sore feet in my dimly lit room, unable to shake the image of the man by the ATM. He'd looked at me like I was someone who allowed herself to be intimate with a stranger. By this point, I was attempting to come to terms with many of the things I had done to support my drug habit. I had tried to keep them buried as I stuffed my feelings down with food. My weight was my camouflage. It hid me from the men in my past who could no longer recognize my larger frame. When I thought about the man at the ATM, I knew I could not hide from what his smug entitlement meant. When I was actively using, heroin took the place of everything. It was my food, my sex, my love. I had no desire to be with any man, but my habit required me to perform. A drug-addicted prostitute is part acrobat, part actress, and part corpse. I was fully aware that I had done these things, yet it was hard to come to terms with the fact that the person who had sold herself—for the same amount I had taken out of the ATM that day—was me. Sooner or later, I would have to come to terms with the fact that I had exchanged sex for money.

Outside my window, I heard the sounds of the Tenderloin. It was full of the hookers, the hustlers, and the violence I escaped when I went into rehab. My walls were scrubbed white, no pictures or posters. There was no carpet, no knickknacks to make things comfortable for me. I was hyper-aware that I was in transition, just like this place. This was not where I wanted to stay in life, but it was all I could handle at the moment.

My needs were simple: a safe place to sleep, a phone call to my mother once a week, a television to watch crime stories that wrapped up neatly at the end of each episode to put me to sleep at night. I was glad to be close to places to eat, because even though there were cooking facilities in my building, I was not sure how to use them. This living situation allowed me to keep my focus on staying clean as my number one priority. The three and a half months I had spent in the program was simply not enough to have a solid foundation for a new life. Eight years of heavy using cannot be erased in forty-two days of intensive treatment. Plus, I had had one foot out the door as soon as I got to rehab—I spent the last half of my stay focusing on working to save enough money to leave. The majority of my healing would need to occur out in the community. The simplicity of my life was a relief, but that relief was rooted in insecurity and fear. I was afraid to do anything other than go to work or meetings because I feared any variation in my pattern would lead to relapse. With the sudden appearance of this man from my past, I could feel the facade begin to tremble as my hands had when I left the ATM that day. I was holding back a mountain of emotions that could fall on me at any moment.

The next morning, I looked through my clothes for something to wear to work. The few pieces I had were hung in perfect alignment. My shoes, all eight uncomfortable pairs of them, were neatly placed at equal distance from each other. Today, especially, everything must be just so for me to be okay with myself.

Standing in front of my meager closet, I tried to push away the thoughts that were making it difficult to get out the door. *Don't wear that, you look ridiculous*, and *Don't call your sponsor, she does not want to hear about your problems*. I changed my clothes hurriedly three times. With each time, the voices were telling me it was not good enough.

Out of pure frustration, I tried to isolate these voices. The main one was that of an old ex-boyfriend. It was not enough that he had abused me in the past. Now, it was as if he was sitting in the room talking to me in that same condescending tone.

He had this intensity about him that made me feel as if he was the only one who mattered. To prove he loved me so much, he got a tattoo of my name. What devotion, right? He separated me from friends who had any doubts about his sincerity, and I became more isolated from everyone except him. Soon it was as if I could do nothing to make him happy. As he constantly reminded me, "Who would want you anyway?" Alone in our apartment, it was me and him and all my mistakes. After he hit me, I finally left him, only to find out he had been sleeping with my friend, validating my deep fear that I was unworthy of love. I ended up homeless and turned to heavy drugs to numb the pain in a matter of weeks of our separation. This was the first time I had reflected on him in years. I had spent so much time in his shadow, I became accustomed to that dark place.

You are worthless. I realized his voice was the main one in my mind. Worthless: The word still echoed in my mind. I would lift up a drink and push down the things he told me. Now I was stone-cold sober. I wished I could tell him to shut up. I hadn't even seen him in nearly a decade. Hadn't I already given him too much time and space? He was the first in the chorus of negativity that had to go. I knew I would have to unravel all the voices before I could trust myself to make good choices. He was the first man who was abusive to me. Unfortunately, more followed. If I was ever going to be happy in my recovery I would have to get emotionally healthy first. I had to find out why I kept repeating the same patterns, expecting different results.

I went to visit one of my former counselors at the treatment facility to ask for help. She had warned me in the past, "When your arms are going around their necks to hug them at those meetings, they are patting your ass." Her observation proved to be dead right.

This time she handed me a sheet of paper and said, "Be selective, sweetie." The paper she gave me directed me to a women-only support group. I took this to mean she didn't think I was ready to make good decisions about men.

When I got to the meeting, I took my place with a small group at a table in the back.

The group leader started by asking us, "What does it mean to be a woman in recovery?"

No one made eye contact with each other, and no one said a word. I recognized the facilitator from my stint in the county jail, when she had first invited me to this group. She had invited me again when I was in residential treatment. When the women would come for her group, the men would snicker, "There goes the hoes." I was not willing to get labeled back then. My attitude was much different now. Huddled there in search of rebuilding our lives, we each had paid a high price for dope, yet no one wanted to be the first one to admit it.

"Who here has had sex for drugs?" she asked. The facilitator was not expecting us to raise our hands. She said it to build identification.

She continued. "Who here had sex with someone and thought you were going to get drugs, but that never happened?" There was a round of nervous laughter. The instant identification washed over us. It was soothing. Yes, I had sex for drugs. Yes, I turned dates thinking I was going to get paid and got ripped off in the process. But who was going to admit these things?

I used plenty of excuses not to connect with people at group meetings. I told myself they couldn't possibly understand. Oh, you don't live outside the facility? Then you aren't like me. You used for twenty years? Something must be seriously wrong with you. You never went to jail? Then what do you know about my situation? If you still have a house and job, clearly we have nothing in common. This ritual was the slow sabotage performed by generations of recovering addicts silently planning a relapse.

If I wanted to stay in the clean and sober world, I must be willing to purge the burden of my past. I took a deep breath and raised my hand.

"My name is Tracey. I am struggling to stay clean." I stumbled on these simple words, but kept going. "I know what this life has in store for me if I go back to using drugs, but I don't know how to go forward, either."

I had no trouble admitting I was a drug addict. Admitting that I had degraded myself for drugs was much more difficult. The same people who could understand a drug arrest became unforgiving when it came to prostitution. How could you *do* that? How could you go *that* far? I wanted to tell them it really wasn't difficult to cross that line. I had slept with a few strangers after a drunken night out at the bars. Why not get paid for it? It seemed like perfect logic. I had a habit to support, these men had their needs. It was mutual usury. I used to repeat a line from Orwell's *1984*: "Under the spreading chestnut tree, I sold you, you sold me." At the time it had seemed like a trade-off, not a compromise. Now I was left feeling alone and ashamed.

I forced the words out into the open: "I had sex for money." There, I said it. It was liberating for me. "I went to the ATM the other day and ran into one of my clients. I was taking out $40—the exact same amount he used to pay me for a blow job."

Once I started talking, I couldn't stop. "I walk by the same spot by City Hall every day. I just want to smash someone's face whenever I walk there." One night I had been walking the street looking for a client. I was off heroin but had taken Klonopin and Xanax to take the edge off, without realizing what would happen when the pills hit me. As I walked through the park in front of City Hall, a man waved me over to the stairwell. "What time is it?" he asked as I approached him. Before I could answer, he pulled out a steak knife and put it to my face.

"I'll do what you want," I said. "Just don't cut my face." I took down my own pants and he clumsily took care of his business. Afterward, he made me sit with him for almost an hour while he smoked crack. He wanted to walk me home like we were on a date. He finally let me leave. I found out later he was a pimp who had been down on his luck that night. I saw him again another time and started yelling, "You motherfucker, I know what you did to me." He took out a gun and stuck it to my head.

"Go ahead, shoot me, kill me," I said. "You'd be doing me a favor."

One of his girls pushed me away and he told her, "This bitch is crazy." Maybe I was out of my mind. Maybe I should have fought for myself instead of letting him take advantage of me without a fight. This was one of the memories I was trying to stuff down. That night on the stairwell came back to me with every attempt to stay clean. On many starless nights, when I felt the most alone, I would go back to that spot. I would take off my backpack. I would pull off my sweatshirt to provide myself with a comfortable seat. I would look over to the spot. They had built a playground there. I would sit there and I would cry. Not a noisy sob, but a suppressed moment of sadness when the tears fell silently. I'd been at this spot when I was twenty-two years old. That was a mere six months after I had come to the city. My life was changed inexorably that night. It was as if every visitor who walked to City Hall trampled on my lost innocence, or perhaps what little innocence I had left by that time.

These were the memories that made it hard to sleep at night. These were the things that had me looking over my shoulder. My new therapist said I had PTSD. She told me I had disassociated that night. My mind and my spirit had left my body. They had protected me from harm. As I faced my life without drugs, it was hard to keep those parts of myself in the same place at the same time. While my body attempted to heal from all the damage, my mind frequently wandered back to that night or other nights I wanted to forget. This group was helping me, but how long could I maintain my sanity when these were the places, people, and memories I passed every day?

When I left the support group, I stepped onto the sidewalk and got a whiff of Popeyes chicken. This whole section of Divisadero smelled like laundry and fried chicken. I decided to grab a few pieces before I got on the bus home.

Some of the other women wanted to walk with me, but I was wary. Women on the street are taught to be competition, not allies. I would have to learn to trust again. For now, I just wanted to be alone. I adjusted my baseball hat. My hair was slicked back into a ponytail. I had on saggy Ben Davis pants, a pressed Ben Davis shirt, a silver chain from my mother, and black Nike Cortez shoes that were hurting my feet even though they were sneakers. These shoes were only for show, anyway. I modeled myself to look like a drug dealer I had admired. I had the air of someone who still ruled the streets and was merely on a substance-free vacation facilitated by the criminal justice system. It was not lost on me that these were the same people I saw pushing a shopping cart or looking for a rock in the gutter. Was I any different? Honestly, who the fuck was I? What was I doing in these clothes and in this place, anyway? I was so raw after the group meeting. I didn't want to cry in public. I blinked as hard as I could and told myself, *Why don't you go home and cry like a little bitch.*

A few months later, after a similar night at my support group, I was waiting alone for the bus with my usual fried chicken. Letting go of some of the most painful parts of my using history had allowed me to come out of my shell. But I was still thankful the Muni bus was not too crowded tonight. It would only be a fifteen-minute ride over the hill to my place. As I headed for an empty seat in the back of the bus, I heard someone call out, "Tracey, is that really you?"

I did not look at the face. I was tired of talking after group, and I knew what was happening here. San Francisco is a small city. It is only seven miles across by seven miles wide. He had seen the HBO movie I was in. It had been out for a few months at this point. From the day the movie aired, my story belonged to the public. And after sharing in group, I was completely opened up and vulnerable. I had told some part of these stories before, just bits and pieces. But this was the first group where I felt comfortable enough to really open up. I could do it in front of a group of women because they *knew* what it was like, which made it less painful somehow. For the first time since I had put down the needle, I was feeling hopeful that perhaps someone could understand the complexities of my sorrow over my choices.

Now here it was again. The past was in my face. The film made it impossible for me to deny what had happened during those years. Six months before it aired, I had made a pilgrimage to Ohio to prepare my family for the worst. It was right before the holidays, and I felt like the ghost of Christmas past returning at the worst time of year. My family was accepting of me despite the fact that we had no common points of reference. I hadn't spent any meaningful time with them since I was a teenager. Now the adults suddenly had gray hair. And I was covered in scars, inside and out. Yet, I was desperate to connect with these people.

My heroin addiction was more than just what happened to me; it was a loss to my family. We were strangers. I was still alive, but in many ways, I no longer existed to them.

I had purposely stopped calling home at one point while I was using. I used to imagine my mother sitting on her green plaid Ethan Allen sofa watching the Lifetime network with her cordless phone next to her on the blanket, waiting for a phone call that never came. Toward the end of my addiction, I had started calling again, and my mother started supplying me with money. I lied and told her I was clean, yet I am certain she heard in my voice that I was on something. By the time I went home for this trip, we had spent many months of Sundays rebuilding our relationship with extended phone conversations. I was no longer calling to ask her for things. I was now providing her with the peace of mind she needed to sleep at night. Finally, she could know I was safe. When I saw her in Ohio I had been away for so long, but to her it was like I had never left. That was because she had never given up the hope that one day the prodigal daughter would finally return home.

One night during my extended stay, the emotions of the day began to overwhelm me. As my family toasted my success, I began to slowly crave the alcohol they enjoyed. The visit was like being in an alternate universe where we were somehow a normal family again. For most of my life, I had seen my mother fight to get my father off alcohol. To see him there slowly sipping a beer as if it was an ordinary event struck me. *What is happening here?* I asked myself. The drinking, the happiness, and the familiarity—which I felt no part of—began to overwhelm me. My family laughed

over events that meant nothing to me. I had no clever stories
of my own to share. As the night wound down, I went upstairs to the guest room in my brother's house. My mouth
was literally watering with cravings for a drink.

I paced back and forth in that guest room. My heart
was in my chest. Maybe I am okay now. Maybe I can have
a drink like everyone else. How is it my father can have a
drink and still have a family? Why is it I am the only one
who can't enjoy a normal evening with a beer in my hand? I
got down on my knees. "God, Buddha, Allah, whoever you
are . . ." I whispered to the universe. "Please don't let me
use—just for today."

In a split second of meditation, my mind became crystal
clear. Yes, some people can work and drink. They can maintain a house, they can maintain a family. But I am not one
of those people. Not me. They will have a few drinks then
go to bed. I knew that I, on the other hand, would have a
few drinks, then a few more, then I would walk out in the
snow to the housing projects to get some crack. Because that
is how my mind works. I don't need to be jealous of what
anyone else can do or have. I simply need to preserve what I
have worked so hard for: peace of mind.

When that man approached me on the bus, he was fucking with my serenity. I had completed a good session with
a powerful group of women. I was in the zone. I felt better
than I would have if I had done two hours on the treadmill.
I had released some of the baggage of my past. I left it at
the door of the meeting. I also was vulnerable. Anytime I
opened up about my feelings, I opened myself up to be hurt.

"Who do you think I am?" I said to the voice on the bus.

I asked myself this question all the time, too. I wondered if, in a crowd full of people, I could be picked out as the addict.

Like a rabbit in a metal trap as the jaws snapped shut on my leg, I heard him say those dreaded words, "You want to get high?"

After exposing my fears at the support meeting, I was feeling so raw, so open, as if someone could walk right into me. I didn't say anything, but I didn't move on either, as I held on to my two-piece-and-biscuit for dear life.

"Well, do you want to get high with me?" He insisted in a louder, determined whisper. "When I saw you in the movie, I thought to myself, there is a person I could get high with. You look really good right now. So healthy."

Healthy. When you get off drugs, "You're so healthy" becomes code for "Look at how fucking fat you are now." When it came to men, my self-esteem was in the toilet. I had to admit that, for a moment, those drugs were sounding more and more appealing to me. This was the moment every heroin addict faces, when your will is tested by an old bag of dope you find in a pocket, a phone call from a dealer, or a sudden feeling of disillusionment when getting high seems a viable option.

I smelled the flesh of my deliciously fried chicken smothered in fatty goodness. I wanted to stuff my face and go to sleep. I wanted to forget my past just long enough to catch my breath. I wished I could pause that moment to sort out what was happening.

Mr. Persistent interrupted my thoughts. "Don't worry. I'll buy." This never happened in real life, but it was happening to me now. I turned to look him in the face. Someone was offering to get me high for free, and he didn't look half bad either.

My mind started to go over the logistics. I couldn't bring him to my place at the transitional house because they would clock him right away as a junkie. I didn't have any syringes. How would I make it to work tomorrow? Would everyone know? These are the kinds of inconsequential things that rush through your mind before you make a bad decision that can change your entire life. My sobriety was just a small piece of the picture. I could lose the trust of others, my job, my housing, or even my life—but I was not thinking of those things. I would not be the first person to be dragged out of sober living in a body bag, all because of a split-second decision.

He reached out to me. I recoiled at the slight brush of the back of his hand. I can never predict what will set off a bad memory. It may be the smell of a certain cologne or the texture of day-old stubble. He touched me like he knew. He thought he could touch me like I was merchandise.

This snapped me out of my daze. Did I want to get high? Hell no. I did not want to get fucking high.

"Are you fucking serious, dude?" I said, brushing past him. "You got the wrong person."

Yes, I'm Tracey. But he had the wrong Tracey. I was not the person he thought he knew. In fact, I was not the Tracey I was at the beginning of 1998. I no longer was the Tracey who went anywhere and did anything to get high. I was stronger than my urges. As much as I wanted to use, I wanted to live even more.

As I jumped off the bus on Market Street, it was a long walk past the rocks at the Civic Center. The ghost of junkies past blew through like cold sea air. I decided I was going to file a police report about my rape. It would be symbolic at this point, but I was tired of having flashbacks and nightmares. I was not going to be silent. I was going to be active in my recovery. I was taking charge of my own self-determination. Yes, that's him. That's the motherfucker right there. I had my voice back, and I was not going to stop talking about my truth. However, at that moment, all I wanted was my fried chicken, damn it. I wanted to eat it at my little table in my room with no bathroom, where I could sit and be myself. I wanted to take off my clothes, which were a sham. I was not scrambling from one high to the next one. I was a woman in recovery. I did not need to be afraid anymore. I just needed to learn how to live.

Chapter 5

THE QUICK FIX

As the months of sobriety passed, I developed a deep sense of gratitude that I had survived eight years of active addiction. The more distance I put between myself and my last hit, the less I wanted to remember. I saw survivors of that life, the few who made it out. I collected their phone numbers knowing I would never use them. I was slowly building new friendships. I wanted to feel as if it was possible for me to start over completely.

One night I was out with some of my new friends. There was a group of four of us. We packed into the corner booth so we could have a space by the window. I loved to people watch in my neighborhood. The best part of the Tenderloin was the intersection of different cultures. I had never noticed when I was buying drugs. There were so many languages, so many different kinds of food. It was like I could be transported to a different place every night. We were enjoying Indian food after our weekly meeting, a young people's group that met on Saturdays in a music space.

I bounced around to different meetings until I found a few that made me feel comfortable. It was just like how I had tried dope from different dealers to find the best stuff; I decided to apply this same principle to recovery. I would often hear complaints from people that they didn't like this meeting or that meeting. They had wanted to give up. The feedback I would give them was simple. If a dealer told you he was sold out, you certainly wouldn't turn around and go home. You would find what you need. Use some of that same determination in recovery. A meeting or support group is only as good as the members. There are some that are better than others. Find what works.

I was feeling confident about this new social circle. I isolated myself most of the time, but I emerged from my protective cocoon a few times a month. I had been slowly opening up over the course of six months. I had almost given up on the idea of friends. It was hard to trust anyone. I had been betrayed so many times before, and I wanted to find a group of people who could just let me be myself. My mother had always said, "In life, you can count all your true friends on one hand." I was working on covering a few fingers. It was nice to feel a part of something outside of work.

One new friend from my clean and sober circle was a few years younger than I. She had more clean time than I, which was part of the attraction. As we talked and laughed, the conversation changed to the neighborhood. She started cracking jokes about a few of the homeless people who shuffled by the window.

I felt a sinking feeling in my stomach when her attention turned to me.

"Have you heard of that new restaurant for the homeless?" she asked.

The others at the table smiled and waited for her response.

She answered, "It's called Tracey-in-the-Box."

Some nervous laughter followed. I was not laughing. My jaw dropped in complete embarrassment. I could not believe what I had just heard. Was she seriously making fun of the fact that I used to be homeless? She was—she really is making a joke of my experience. I didn't know whether I should throw my Diet Coke can at her head or cry. I wanted to be invisible.

As I slid down in the booth, she tried to apologize. But the damage was done. *Even among people in recovery I am a fucking freak*, I thought. Time to find a new meeting.

Instead of trying to escape my past, I decided I should find someone who could relate to me. At different points in my recovery, I have searched for different things. As my recovery matured, I became less interested in how I appeared to other people and more concerned with how I saw myself. I had done a considerable amount of damage. I needed to find out where my fellow former low-bottom users hung out. Those who had worked their way up from the very bottom and gotten their lives together. I would have to find a way to make it work.

I hadn't seen Cat for a few months. I used to go to a meeting where she was a regular, but my schedule had changed since I took on a few shifts a month teaching overdose prevention to anyone who would listen to me. This was in addition to my full-time job at an outpatient program. In the way I had become addicted to so many other things in my life, I was finding myself becoming addicted to work. I would take on any additional shifts or tiresome projects, and even agreed to out-of-town travel. I hated spending too much time alone in my room. It gave me too much time to think about things I did not want to remember. Staying busy was my new fix. Between work, more work, meetings, and weekly dental appointments to get my teeth fixed, I felt the safety of a routine. The Saturday meeting was perfect for my schedule, but after the incident at the restaurant, I needed a break. Unfortunately, the Wednesday meeting, the meeting where I would see Cat, had been bumped from the schedule.

I would not describe Cat as a close friend. We were happy to see one another, for sure, but we never went out on social excursions. We had more of a mutual appreciation society. During the two years when I had lived on the street with all my belongings in a shopping cart, Cat and her former boyfriend were frequent campmates of mine. She had known "Tracey-in-the-Box" and still liked me. Her boyfriend was much older, much more seasoned, and frequently abusive to her. He would sway back and forth. We could see that the meth made him more and more agitated to the point he would sometimes literally foam at the mouth in the middle of one of his rages. He hated me. I hated him even more. When he smacked her, it was generally away from anyone who could intervene, not that anyone would have stopped him. We all had our own problems.

I was dealing with abuse in my own relationship at the time, one that drove me to attempt suicide. I tried to kill myself one afternoon by throwing myself into the ocean. As I was feeling the dark pull of the icy water, I suddenly came to the realization that the thing I wanted most in the entire world was to keep breathing. I wanted to live. I eventually got myself to shore, as strangers circled me to help. I didn't want them to touch me. I accepted a ride back to my encampment, shoeless, shivering, and afraid my boyfriend would be angry at what I had done. Cat was the first person to wrap a blanket around me. She helped me as I returned to the edge of the alley, and she didn't ask me a bunch of questions. As she pulled a spare pair of socks from her backpack, I could tell by the look in her eyes reflected in the streetlight that she had been in the same place. She did not know what exactly had happened that day. She didn't need to know all the details. She understood the pain I was in and that was enough: the pain of a life of misery that never seemed to end. Now, when I would see her in the meetings, she would touch my leg and smile. She held the same strength it took for both of us to finally break free. That feeling of quiet connection without judgment was what I needed.

The next time I heard from her, I knew the news was not good. I was curled up on my bed with my big fluffy green alien pillow and my detective shows. The phone rang behind my head, breaking my concentration.

"Hi, this is Tracey," I answered, as if I was still chained to my desk at work. I was irritated by the interruption. I loved my forensic files. I kept waiting to see people I knew on this show. In some ways, it was a manifestation of vicarious trauma, but I couldn't stop myself.

"Hey, Tracey," I heard a familiar voice on the other end. "This is Cat."

An unexpected call from another person in recovery is rarely a good thing. I had learned these calls only mean one thing.

She continued. "I'm calling about Jake."

She didn't need to finish the sentence—I knew. Jake was dead. Fuck.

Jake had been in the documentary with me, and one of the few friends Cat and I had had in common. The last I knew, he had gotten out of perhaps an even worse place than where we had been. He was the type of person who could make friends easily and lose them quickly. His desire for friends made him generous with his time, his space, and his drugs. I had needed that in my life. I remembered many afternoons sitting in the warm sun nodding off with Jake next to me. I knew he'd had some type of crush on me at some point. Then on other days he hated me. That was just the way we were together. One night at the corner store, he asked to take a picture of me. He wanted to hang it up in his room. He wanted to keep some part of me with him.

He was the only person I knew who could remain stable enough to keep an address. He was nice enough to let me use it for a court release program. Sometimes I came over and slept on his floor. Other times, we sat silently together in the doorway while we were both between hustles. More than anyone I knew in my many years of using, Jake had wanted to be loved. On one of the many occasions we had been out in the elements waiting for money to appear in the form of a "date," the song "Creep" by Radiohead was playing next to us. As Jake sang along, I felt a chill go up my spine. It was as if the words fit him perfectly; the words still echo in my mind whenever I think of him.

Things had changed so dramatically for Jake since the last time I had passed him in one of our alleys. We had drifted apart during the last year of my using, each of us dealing with the fallout of the HBO movie in our own way. I saw some of the others from the film here and there. Life after it came out was much harder for some of them than what I had experienced. No one was hounding me or looking down on me because of my HIV status, like what happened to another woman in the film. The distance between me and the Tracey in the movie was much more pronounced.

One day I'd been casually flipping through a message pad at the outpatient program at my day job when a name caught my eye. There was a message that read: "Looking for a job—Jacob B." That seemed so odd to me. I had to follow up with one of my coworkers. Yes, she confirmed, not only was Jake clean, he was looking for work. To see his name on that notepad, looking for a job, made me feel like maybe there really was hope for all of us.

I didn't call him that day. But it made me feel better knowing he was around and looking for work. It made me feel like some part of my past had resolved itself. I saw him a few months later when he was volunteering. He was a door-man at Gilman, an all-ages club in Berkeley. It was a shock to see him. He had put on weight. His face was round and healthy. There was a twinkle in his eyes. It was easy for him to smile and laugh, not like the Jake I had known. He was healthy. It was like a dream.

"You live with roommates?" I asked as he stamped my hand as proof of payment.

He spoke with a southern twang from his years in Alabama.

"Yep, I finished treatment," he told me. "I got a place."

He checked in a few other customers and stamped their hands. These people coming here looked like babies compared to the way Jake and I had looked in our early twenties. We had already been hardened by the world at that point. These twenty-somethings were sneaking in bottles of booze shoved down their pants so they could go swill it in the bathroom. By the time Jake and I were twenty-one, we were already junkies. We smiled at each other with the knowledge that they would never be like us. They looked too fucking happy just to be here.

"I got a girlfriend, too," he said casually, "and I'm finally getting off that methadone."

That seemed odd. *If it isn't broke, don't fix it,* I thought. If the methadone was helping him maintain some stability for the first time in his adult life, why go off it? I thought of my own precariousness during those crucial first weeks and months of recovery, how I was terrified to change anything for fear I'd relapse. It scared me that Jake was about to make a big change to his routine.

He explained, "Everyone says I am not really clean because I am on methadone. I go to meetings here. I am almost off."

Well, who the fuck was "everyone"? Certainly not people who knew Jake. They may have met him since he had left treatment, but they didn't know where he came from. They never shared a blanket with him curled up in a ball in a freezing parking garage, trying to dodge leaks from the ceiling. They never saw him cry because someone had abused him. What did "everyone" know? My heart sank. So many things I wanted to say, but I bit my tongue and promised to see him inside. We didn't have time for the things I wanted to say to him. We didn't have time for me to shake him by the shoulders. I wanted to tell him, "Fuck what everyone else thinks. You are clean. You are in recovery. You are a living example of recovery if I ever saw one." We didn't have time for me to tell him, "Hey, this is the best you have ever done since you started using so long ago. *Please* don't fuck this up." But we just ran out of time.

I understood how he felt to a certain extent. From the day I moved back to the Tenderloin and into the sober living environment, I had received an endless stream of opinions about my living situation. "You should move out of there" seemed to be the consensus among anyone and everyone I came across who heard about my living situation. The problem was that I never asked them for their opinion. They felt free to offer their advice without knowing anything about my situation. I knew I was in the right living situation for me. My decision was personal. I had sponged off my parents for so long, my self-esteem increased exponentially with each day I was self-sufficient. I needed to stay within my means, keep my world small, and focus on getting better. I had seen too many of my peers fall into the trap of moving too quickly. The pattern went like this: move out of treatment, move in with roommate, roommate relapses, they relapse. Or they found a partner and the partner relapsed. The End. My path was my own, and I was just fine.

Jake heard the same kind of advice. He was like me, except he did not know when to tune people out. It is hard for people who are in the early stages of recovery. We want to *believe* that these people in the meetings want the best for us. They certainly hug us and tell us that they care for us. But in my heart, at that moment, on that day at Gilman, I just *knew* this was wrong for him. I just couldn't articulate my feelings. Not only was it not my place, but I wanted him to be right. I wanted him to have the type of recovery that he idolized—abstinence-based recovery, the type found in twelve-step, without medications. I just didn't believe it could work for him. There is no quick fix for people like us. We need years to recover, not months. As they say in the clichés, some people are just sicker than others.

About a month or so after seeing Jake at Gilman, I was walking down Market Street in the center of the San Francisco shopping district when I saw a familiar figure on the sidewalk. For whatever reason, I recognized those feet. Jake was the only person to wear sandals in any kind of weather. He had been picking at his skin as if he was doing stimulants, and he had red scabs all over. He was wearing the same sweatshirt from the last time I saw him at Gilman, except now it was dirty and cut up at the neck.

"I fucking relapsed," he told me.

A few weeks after he had gotten off methadone, he had started using again.

"Just go back to the clinic, Jake," I told him with urgency. I tried to be supportive. The people swirling around us gave us cold stares. They didn't know the story behind the faces. They just had somewhere to go. And so did I—I was rushing to get to another work site. Never, for one second, did I believe this would be the last time I would talk to him. He closed his eyes to feel the sun on his face. I encouraged him to get off the street, one last time.

As I listened to Cat go over all the details of Jake's death, I got angrier and angrier. Jake had been dead for a few days in the room that he had rented before some people from the program asked the police to kick in the door. The people who knew him from his using days struggled over why this had happened. I personally believed it was much more than the "disease of addiction." This was something far more manmade. Why had people meddled in his life? Why did it matter to them if he was "clean" according to their standards? I had known this man. I had known his struggles. Why did they take someone who was so impressionable, someone who wanted so much to be liked, and make him believe there was something wrong with his recovery?

I rarely went to memorial services. At this early stage in my recovery, death was too painful. Throughout my addiction and early recovery, I had known many people who died. My best friend had died from AIDS-related complications when I'd been in jail a few years earlier. I'd found out when a letter I sent to him was returned to me. It was stamped

"Deceased." That was it—no explanation, just a declaration that my friend Mark was gone. I wasn't able to be there for his service, but I made up my mind: I would go to Jake's. Cat agreed to give me a ride. As we approached the site of his memorial, it felt surreal. It was held at the same place I'd seen him that last night. The club was brighter and open without music-goers packed inside. I sat on one of the soiled couches. They were covered in graffiti. Jake had felt at home here. I felt so uncomfortable. I looked around the room. I wondered who had been the one to tell him he wasn't clean. Was it more than one person? Were they crying because they felt guilty, or were they clueless in righteous justification? Is being "clean" more important than being alive? I wanted to implicate them all in his death. Maybe I had been just as guilty somewhere along the way. I had also thought at one point that twelve-step was the only "true" recovery. Now I was converted. There must be alternatives, I thought, and I needed to find them. On the way back, Cat handed me a few of Jake's belongings. They had been divided among his friends.

Cat and I only saw each other a few times after that evening. She had school, I had school. Life was a constant series of people moving in and out of my life. Recovery works like that sometimes. Because I had a clear mind, I appreciated the gift of having a few special moments with a person.

I made a choice for myself as a direct result of Jake's death. I wanted to find a way to work in harm reduction in a more in-depth way. I wanted to advocate for people to be treated with respect and dignity as they made their own personal choices about their substance use. For the first time since I had quit drugs in 1998, I was beginning to see that twelve-step could actually be harmful for some people. I began to realize that advice is not the same thing as facts. I wanted to know more facts. Opinions create advice and advice causes people to think they are experts.

Whether it was personal or professional, everyone with a little bit of clean time seemed to think of themselves as experts. When I started my first counseling, I was very vocal about practicing an abstinence-based program. I thought I was an expert as well. We were told that if we had six months clean, we had something to offer the person who had six days. So I naturally assumed I was in a position to pass along "facts" hidden in advice based on what had helped me. At the time, I was counseling sexual abuse survivors with substance abuse issues at the outpatient program. I had nine months clean, and I was thrown into the deep end of the pool with people who had been suffering multiple kinds of trauma. My days were full of tales of rape, prostitution, child molestation, and other assorted horror stories. It made it difficult to sleep at night. But I wanted to make a difference in the world. I thought, naïvely, *If I can only get these clients off drugs, everything will be great!* Abstinence, I thought, must be the only way that worked. It worked for me; it must work for you. I really thought I was helping people by preaching the gospel I was taught in twelve-step.

But it was just that: my personal experience. It did not make me an "expert," just another person with an opinion. Before I had any professional training, I fell into another pitfall of the peer counseling world. I thought my job was an extension of my recovery. That made me heavy on the advice and short on the listening. I had an idea of what I wanted for the clients. They might have wanted something completely different. I was completely unaware of all the complexities of their situations because I was so focused on the outcome I wanted for them. For some people, drugs are their protection. Drugs are their only coping mechanism. Drugs are what keep them alive. To completely abandon their self-medication means dealing with realities they might not be able to handle. After a few people I knew had gotten clean only to commit suicide, I began to question my own motives. I sought out more training, more supervision, and began to listen more. I learned to practice compassionate detachment. I was there to witness the pain of others, not to make decisions for them. I learned the "what worked for me" model could detract from the healing process. These were not my wounds I needed to heal. I needed my own process of recovery; they needed theirs. I chose to learn from Jake's death, and it made me a better counselor.

In the first few years, my personal recovery was rigid. I came home after a long day of work. The work was draining me. I needed to go to a meeting. Or did I, I wondered. I lay on my bed one night, my mind spinning. What if I was wrong about twelve-step? What if I was investing all my time and energy in some cultish bullshit? Was I like Jake, the person who could never use again, or was I like the person who can have a little drinkie poo every now and then? Here I was with clean time, living below my means in a piss-in-the-sink hotel in a shitty section of town in one of the most beautiful cities in the world. Maybe I was making a mistake. What if I just finished school, got my own place, put my past completely behind me? I could go hang out with people after work. I could get some drinks, smoke some weed. I could be "normal" again.

These thoughts continue to scare the shit out of me, even now from time to time. I start to let myself daydream about my new life. I imagine myself going out for a drink with my new "normal" friends. Then reality sets in. How does this scenario play out? I have two drinks, then four, then I lose count. Then I wander down the street and get some heroin. I sneak off to some enclave. No one will know, and I deserve this one time. The night ends with me in an ambulance or the coroner's office. Because—that is the way my using goes. It is simply how I am. Jake taught me that. There are people who can do "just one more." Then there are people like us.

When I feel slightly bitter about the fact that I may never have a drink again, I think about how blessed I really am. A drink seems pretty insignificant in comparison to the life I have now. Why take the risk? I have evidence that some people can return to appropriate alcohol use after they quit heroin. I just don't believe I am one of those people. I never drank for the taste. When I see someone out at dinner nursing what he or she must be thinking is delicious beer for thirty minutes, I think to myself, *For fuck's sake—are you going to finish that?* And to see someone walk away and leave some in a glass is almost unbearable. I have a long history of seeking that instant gratification. When I would read a book, I'd flip to the ending. When I went on a diet, I liked to starve myself into losing ten pounds in a month. When I would meet a person I liked, I skipped the courtship and went straight to sex. I don't bother with dinner if I can get away with eating a whole cake. I am a person of extremes. I enjoy the quick fix. I want joys without sorrow. I want love without the questions. Whatever I was using, I just wanted results.

I eventually learned that I can be flexible without crossing the complete abstinence bar I set for myself. I can learn, I can change, I can evolve. I need to stay connected to my past to learn from it. I accepted that I would not shy away from my history. Instead, I would use it to become more accepting of others. There are many roads to the same destination. I needed to be accepting of my own path. Recovery is not what other people expect from me. It is about the choices I make for myself. I only had to give up one thing—drugs— and in return I got a chance at everything.

Chapter 6

A NEW SENSE OF SELF

When I first got into rehab they told me there was only one thing I needed to change: everything. I resented this idea that there was nothing about me that could be salvaged in my new life. I felt like deep down inside I was a good person. My behavior did not always reflect my beliefs, but that was the result of being chained to substances that overpowered my best intentions. Was there nothing that made me lovable? Was it me who made those decisions, or was it the heroin whispering in my ear? Learning to trust myself and my motives was a long uphill climb. I could lotion up my track marks, get some new clothes, and experiment with makeup. But none of that changed the way I felt about the person inside the wounded body. In rehab, they told me I was sick—that I had a disease. I wondered if I was broken. Why else would I have lied, cheated, and compromised myself for drugs? I needed much more than a few months in a controlled environment to believe I was a good person. I needed to work on myself on a daily basis, chipping away at the barriers to my new sense of self.

Self-loathing was nothing new to me. The drugs served a purpose. They silenced that voice inside my mind that told me I was worthless. It didn't take much for that ex-boyfriend to convince me that that was true; I had long believed in my worthlessness. Much of this feeling had focused on my weight issues. Besides stuffing myself to drown my problems, before I found drugs I had made the rounds of other kinds of self-destructive behaviors. There were the eating disorders, there was the cutting. In my late teens, I tried puking, laxatives, enemas, and blood pressure medicine to lose weight. When I was on drugs, I was validated for being skinny. For the first and only time in my life, I could try on a bikini and it fit. True, the only place I ever got to wear it was one time next to my shopping cart, but in my warped thinking that didn't matter—I could fit into a bikini. When I got back out into the free world after jail, putting on weight, no longer feeling numb, hearing those voices again drove me into a deep depression. I needed to find other outlets besides trying to control my appearance.

The real work on myself started at the residential facility. It was as if the clock started ticking on my adulthood when I got through those doors. I was transferred from jail—I was brought in wearing handcuffs. At least they left the leg shackles off. When the sheriff handed me off to the facility, they made it clear that I was still the property of the county until I completed my sentence—that I wouldn't "escape" until I was released from rehab. So much for the idea of a heartwarming pep talk about how I was going to make it.

Within a few days of entering rehab, I would start getting a few privileges. In a little over a month, with good behavior, I would be expected to find a job. Unlike many of the residents, I had done some "programming" during my jail stay. I was familiar with groups and the lingo. I was fully detoxed off drugs. I had a few months of living clean under my belt. It was not unusual to get roommates who were fresh from the street and detoxing on their bunks. The doors only locked from the outside, so you could leave any time of the day or night—you just couldn't get back in. Once that door closes, they'd remind us, you will be on your own. Many residents would disappear without notice, leaving the staff to pack up their belongings in case they or their families ever returned to collect what had been left behind.

I had very little when I arrived at the door. I was discharged from jail in the same pajamas I had worn the night I was arrested. Now they were extra tight, since I'd gained fifty pounds while in jail. Luckily, the program provided me with a few clothing items to get me started—some flannel shirts, T-shirts, and Levi's were all I needed to try to blend into the background. I also had a few dollars, my rings, and a stack of letters from my mother. She had written me two or three times a week while I was inside.

When I go back in my memory, though, the work on myself really started with a phone call a few months after I'd arrived. "Did I get a call today?" I asked the woman at the front window one day. I was waiting for a call back about an application for a job. We were allowed to use a special phone line that did not scream "REHAB" when potential employers called for us.

She smiled at me as she handed me a slip of paper. "Yes," she said, "here you go, Tracey."

The staff here were a combination of jailer and therapist. I found it humiliating to have to piss in a cup in front of them every week for random drug tests, then have to socialize with the same person an hour later. But the tests had their merit. I had heard other residents say how they had decided not to use during their passes home because they were so concerned about getting tested when they got back. A dirty test would have sent me back to jail for six months. I tried to remember that when I handed over my cup. The woman at the desk was tall, an imposing size, and doubled as a counselor to the women. There were so few of us there that we were not even entitled to a full-time staff person. She was a lesbian, a proud one at that. For whatever reason, this made me feel better about her. I felt like she would not judge me about my own sexual experiences with women. There was another counselor who was super-Jesus-churchy. I would never have told her my personal details. Religion may work for some folk, but the only times I ever came close to praying were when I was in jail, or I was broke and needed a fix. *Please God, help me find this vein.* Those four years at Catholic school did nothing but make me more jaded. My parents sent me there hoping they would keep me off drugs. Instead, I learned about drugs for the first time from my classmates.

I opened up the piece of paper the staff person had handed me. It wasn't what I was expecting. "Call me. Mom."

I was waiting for a call back from Goodwill for a job I had applied for a few weeks before. I should have heard something by then. I figured they were just not going to call me. The fucking GOODWILL was not going to call me! This would have been a blow to my fragile ego if I didn't find it so hilarious. I had two and a half years of college. I couldn't get a call back to stock fucking racks at a job training program? I shook my head. I would have laughed, except I really needed money. I had my job at the market research place, but I was hoping this might pay a little more.

I slipped down the hallway in the women's living area to the pay phone. It only took my mother two rings to pick up. She must have had her cordless phone next to her. She had started sleeping in the living room when my father started drinking heavily. I was twelve years old at the time. It was strange to watch TV in my room because my mother was sleeping out in the common area. Eventually, the abnormal became normal to me. I wasn't isolating upstairs—I was just giving her space. I didn't need to interact with anyone. Now, despite having three empty bedrooms after her children moved out, she was still sleeping in the living room. I freely admitted to anyone willing to listen that I didn't understand my parents' relationship. I assumed they had some bond I couldn't see. Why else would she have hung on all these years? My mother had her ways of coping with pain, and I had mine. She still watched her Lifetime movies at night, fell asleep with the phone next to her, and waited on phone calls from her children.

"Hey Mom," I said, leaning into the wall next to the pay phone. "What's up?"

I could hear the fatigue in her voice. My mother was often weary from the weight of the world.

"Hey, I was just dozing here," she said. "What time is it there?"

It was six o'clock in San Francisco, meaning she was tucked in before nine o'clock Ohio time. The burden of a lifetime of dealing with addiction and mental illness in her family had worn her down. My mother had been wedged between our vices and imperfections. Sometimes it seemed that she was the only normal one. Her big personality was, in some ways, a facade. Like other women of her generation, she knew how to put on a happy face. She was simply better at hiding her anxieties and phobias than much of the rest of the world. She was afraid of so many random things: riding in cars, traveling into big cities, and thunderstorms. I was told my mom used to drag me into a closet if she heard the loud crash of seasonal thunder. I inherited that anxiety. It was as if she was always vaguely afraid of something. I understood how that felt. She had found her own unique ways to cope. Some people lean into their fears, absorb them as part of being human. My mother found every way humanly possible to avoid or suppress them. She was like a loaded spring that never got to release all that pent-up energy.

"I need to take a shower before the evening meeting,

Mom. I don't have much time," I explained. "I got your message. What is so important that you needed to call the front desk?"

I could hear her let out a sigh. It was a sigh of disappointment. Now that I was not on drugs, I wasn't as dependent on her. This was the sick truth between us. I don't think she planned for this dynamic between us—it just happened along the way. She liked that feeling of knowing I would always need her for something. For the first few years in San Francisco, I rarely contacted her. When she was willing to provide financial help, it created a lifeline between us. Now I was trying to do something completely on my own, and it scared her. She didn't want to lose me again.

"Well . . ." she hesitated. "I am going to the post office tomorrow. Did you need me to send you anything?"

My response was quick. "Nope."

There was an awkward pause. I could tell this was not what she wanted to hear.

"I don't need anything, Mom," I responded.

I felt like I was ten years old again. "I got a job now. I want to try to do things on my own."

She interrupted me. "Well . . . yes. But I am still your mother."

She wanted to help me somehow. I suppose I was hard to reach. Not only did I live two thousand–plus miles away, I was somewhat emotionally frozen toward the world, including her. The only way she knew how to help me was by buying me things or giving me cash. I found it hard to take any life advice from her seriously. I guess I have never gotten over the fact that she stayed with my father. How could nine and a half years of Al-Anon end in a place where she still put up with his bullshit? I just didn't understand it. It tainted any other type of wisdom she tried to give me.

My parents had sat me down at the kitchen table when I was twelve or thirteen years old to tell me they were going different ways. It was quite a dramatic affair. I knew they fought every single day; it just seemed unbelievable that they would *finally* call it quits. They were supposed to be talking to me, but it was as if they were speaking to each other. I stared at the floor as they talked above me, looking at one another as they spoke. "Well, your mother thinks . . ." It made me feel as if I did not exist. I just wanted to disappear. As they were describing to me the ways their separation would not impact me, for whatever reason I took a steak knife from the center of the table and started rubbing the serrated edge back and forth against the skin on my leg until it started to bleed. "Blah blah blah" was all I heard. The pain was a pleasant distraction. That wasn't the first time I had done some type of self-mutilation—I used to poke myself with safety pins. I have no recollection of when I started this behavior; I only knew it distracted me from what was going on around me. My father stopped me eventually, but it took him at least ten minutes to notice. The whole incident was a metaphor for my relationship with my parents. The two of them were so entangled in their own personal drama that it made me feel invisible. In the end, nothing much came of the conversation. My father started traveling frequently for work. My mom started going to Al-Anon. My father's drinking was never given as a reason for their separation, which was never addressed. It was the specter that haunted all of our relationships. As with many things in my life, there was no resolution.

My mom was always left holding things together. Talking to her on the phone that day, I didn't want to be a burden any longer. I didn't want her to help me anymore. I made a conscious decision that, for the first time in my life, I wanted to do things solely on my own.

That decision changed the course of my life. I had never been completely self-reliant. I used other people as my crutch. I had always relied on someone to fix me. Incrementally, I had learned to pass my personal control over to someone close to me. I felt like a failure at being myself; why not let someone else choose for me? It made it easy to feel sorry for myself because I never had to take personal responsibility for anything. That made an easy segue into addiction. I was never to blame. It was never my fault. "If x person hadn't done x" was my mantra. I was a righteous junkie. Now, at twenty-eight years old, I needed to take my power back. I wanted to be in charge of my life. It was the only way to repair my broken self-esteem. I had to believe I could take care of Tracey. In the previous few months, I had gotten glasses, started getting my teeth fixed, and opened a bank account with no cosigner. I was the boss and it felt good.

When I was in high school, my parents gave me one piece of advice for my future: Study law or business.

"What about psychology?" I had asked.

Their response was definitive. NO.

My parents had their own idea about what it meant to be successful in this world. They were not planning on wasting their hard-earned money on just any degree—they wanted me to get one that would provide a return on their investment. My father had once told me about how, when he was in high school, he refused to drop out to get a job at the local grocery store, so my grandfather refused to go to his graduation, the first ever in the family. The lack of support and guidance at home was always a painful memory for my father. He had joined the Navy to get out of poverty. He worked hard to provide us with all the material things he thought we needed. As the one who paid for those material things, he felt he was also the person who should make the decisions. After his one (unsuccessful) trip to counseling for alcohol abuse, I suspect he felt strongly that counseling was a fairly useless profession.

Money—and the control that it gave my father—was always a point of contention in our house. He frequently belittled the work my mother performed. His ego never recovered from the fact that my mother chose to work rather than stay at home. She knew that having her own income would give her some independence. Both my parents wanted me to be successful for different reasons. My father wanted me to be successful because it would be an extension of his sacrifices; my mother knew economic freedom would allow me mobility. They were clear on one thing, though: no psychology degree for me. They would not allow it.

She adamantly declared, "With a business degree, you can do anything!"

I rolled my eyes in disapproval.

"You can major in psychology," she told me. "We just won't pay for it."

This was one of the few times I saw the two of them agree on anything.

I ended up taking some psychology classes with a business concentration. It seemed like a good compromise: I wanted to learn about what motivates people. I wanted to know what motivated me. Living my life as an outsider, I became excellent at reading people. At first it was for self-preservation. Later, it was because I was genuinely interested in what influenced various behaviors. Over the course of my life, I had tried retail, food service, and office work, but I knew these jobs would never make me happy. I had to find a job that challenged me every day. I had to take the steps to make that possible.

Even before I stopped sticking a needle in my arm, I knew I needed to find a way to go back to college. It was one of the dreams that kept me alive. School was the part of my life where I felt like I fit in—I felt important there. Before, I had used my body to survive. Now I wanted to use my mind. After years of heavy drug use, this would be no easy task. At times, it was hard for me to put a sentence together. The drugs, especially my years of heavy stimulant use, seemed to rob me of my short-term memory. But I was willing to try. I would certainly lose it—permanently—if I never tried to use it. School would be a way to restore what I had lost. I was ready to start the process to go back.

I met with counselors at rehab to start the long road back to school. They had good news for me: It had been so long since I had worked, my low income would allow me to get grants that would cover some form of higher education in California. This was the only time in my life when poverty had been an asset. I needed the help. Despite working full time, I had barely been able to afford the costs of moving out into sober living. I had to fill out what seemed like a thousand forms to apply for financial aid; I didn't even bother to apply to schools until I had done that. Without aid, there would be no college. I knew this. As I slowly worked my way through the financial aid form, I saw "the box," as I would again and again, on various forms throughout my recovery life: "Have you ever been convicted of a felony?" Yes! Yes I had. Ouch. The counselor explained that because I had completed rehab there would be a follow-up question allowing me to explain, where I could essentially say, "Hey, I'm a felon—but I am a druggie who completed rehab! Yay!" No matter what I tried to do, I was constantly having to explain myself to strangers. I could see why people in recovery gave up.

Once I filled out the forms for financial aid, it was time to figure out where I could take classes. The whole process seemed like a comedy of errors. Each person I tried to get information from had only part of the story. In total, I met with six different people at three different places. The community college directed me to apply to San Francisco State University, since, given my prior course load, I was too far into a four-year degree to start there. I later learned this was not true. I could have saved myself $5,000 in grants and loans by taking classes at community college, then transferring to a four-year college. Instead, I would be jumping into the deep end of the pool. I felt like I was seventeen again. I was barely keeping my head above water.

After filling out *more* forms, I got a letter in the mail from SFSU to bring my transcripts to the new student orientation. My transcripts? Fuck—I hadn't even thought about that. They wouldn't take the word of a convicted felon? I needed an official record of the work I had completed at the University of Cincinnati. I needed my mother to help me get my immunization records. I needed papers proving I had completed high school. These tasks were stacking up. I had lost every piece of my identity over the past ten years. I lost all my yearbooks, my class ring, all my pictures, all my writings, all my belongings, and most of my dignity. It was almost as if I did not exist between 1988 and 1998, then reappeared with the fears of a teenager and the problems of an addicted adult. With the exception of the documentary, there were no photographs of me. The only records of my existence were mugshots and my "rap sheet"—my criminal record.

When I received my transcripts, I braced myself for the damage as I ripped open the envelope. During that last semester alone, I had been shooting heroin, cocaine, and MDMA in between drinking binges. My cumulative GPA was much lower than I had expected: a solid C minus. This was for a person who had started nearly a year ahead of her peers. My last quarter: *Incomplete, Incomplete, D, B.* Hmm. I was surprised to see a B there. Maybe I wasn't the only person on drugs while I was in that school. Any teacher who would give me a B in that last quarter did not give a fuck about higher education. It was that bad.

As the night of the orientation at SF State approached, I started to get excited about my future. My shitty market research job paid the bills. I was grateful for that, but I knew it certainly was not a career. I didn't want to be that forty-year-old asshole who calls during dinner to try to get people to answer questions about their political opinions. I saw my future in that room. There was the fifty-plus-year-old alcoholic who worked as Santa for cash at Christmas. There were drag queens, senior citizens, and more than a few people starting over like myself. There was the overweight ginger with the two-foot-long mullet. There was the punk rock burnout dude who worked here to pay the bills.

Men in rehab seemed to have more luck than women. They got into jobs in the trades—most of these started at nearly double the minimum wage—often before they had even finished rehab. Over and over again, I saw men in the program get hired despite lengthy criminal records. Women seemed to fall into retail or service jobs, which made it much more difficult to obtain stable housing without working two jobs. And the men had mentors. There were social clubs for men in recovery, breakfast meetings, and special groups set aside to address their needs for reentry into society. From my perspective, it seemed like society wasn't prepared to deal with women with substance abuse issues. Since men were seen as breadwinners, everything was geared toward getting them back to work, yet women were frequently the sole supporters of their children and family members. If the best way to get a job was to know someone, the women certainly fell behind before they even got started back into the world. School would give me a new set of advantages. I needed to get in before I got lost.

I boarded the packed train that would take me out to the university for orientation on a cold January evening. It seemed like everyone on the train was a student. In that moment, I felt like I belonged there. I was going to school! There was a feeling in the pit of my stomach, like butterflies. I felt like I was going on a first date. I really, really hoped they would like me. As I walked across the campus, I felt a spring in my step. I had bought a shiny new backpack for the occasion, a nice one that wouldn't feel too heavy when I loaded it down with fifty pounds of books. I planned on taking classes part time while working full time. My commute to and from work would only be ten minutes, so I could use the extra time to study. I wanted to start off slowly, and I had browsed the course catalog to select classes that would allow me to do that. The three months of forms and appointments had prepared me for this evening.

Inside, I took my seat at one of the round tables. The orientation quickly breezed through the things I needed to know to graduate. I liked the fact that I was able to take a few classes I wanted before I had to decide on a major. SF State used a semester system, unlike my last school, which was on a quarter system. This left room for some (though not many) electives. I was picturing myself here. I was much older than most of the students, yet I still saw a few people my age in the room. I heard my name called. It was time to see the advisor.

As I walked up to the table, I felt myself burst with pride.

"Name, please," said the man. He had a nondescript face and a cheap sweater.

The computers were lined up against the wall. Five advisors per five students in a row of tables.

"Tracey Lynne Helton," I told him.

I saw my name printed on a stack of papers. He checked my name off his list.

He asked briskly, "Did you bring your transcript to complete your file?"

I sheepishly handed him my transcripts. He flipped through them a few times.

Immediately, I saw there was a problem. He handed them back to me.

"You don't meet the minimum requirements," he told me in a matter-of-fact tone. "You need to have a GPA of 2.5 or higher to transfer here."

I felt the color draining out of my face. The world was in slow motion. I saw people lining up for their tour of the campus. They were all laughing at me. While they'd been going to community college, I was busy sucking dick for heroin. I was standing there in front of all those fucking people, being told I was completely worthless. I shoved my papers in my bag. He was trying to explain other things to me, things I couldn't hear. I couldn't hear anything except indistinct talking sounds. *They must be saying I'm plugging up the line*, I thought. Any of those normal people could have been in my place.

As I turned away, I felt my face getting hot and wet. I wasn't sure what it was at first. I was so angry with myself. It took a minute to realize those were tears. This was the first time I had cried since I stopped using heroin. The last time was over a spilled hit of dope. The cooker got too hot. It started to burn my friend's hand. He wasn't tough enough to hold the burning metal. He let it go and most of my drugs spilled into the gutter. All of my hopes and dreams had been inside that cooker. I was sick. He spilled my drugs on top of piss and garbage. The brown liquid evaporated like my soul leaving my body. I felt the tears explode from my eyes. I had felt so miserable that day. Just like how I felt right now.

I was incredibly embarrassed. I had that feeling when you say something so stupid you want to rip off your mouth and shove it in your pocket. I was hurt. I was the kind of hurt that made me want to break something. I was so tired of fighting to be just as good as everyone else. I could not stop crying, snot and tears rushing down my face. I had to walk fifteen minutes across the campus, wait fifteen minutes for the train, and spend twenty more minutes riding to my stop. Something was released inside me. I could not hold back the tears. I gave people a look, daring them to say something to me. I didn't have the strength to hold down my feelings for one second longer. I had finally imploded with a rush of emotions. The loss of heroin had left a huge hole in my life. Heroin had provided the complete suspension of reality I needed. Without it, life seemed like an impossible task. Back then, when I had woken up every morning, I knew heroin was my purpose. I needed to get the drugs that would make me feel better. Now, I was drifting in an unfamiliar ocean. I was clean, yes, but I was not cured. I still wanted the feeling drugs gave me. The people in the meetings must have been brainwashed. Could they actually be happy without ever taking a drug again? Why was life so hard? I didn't remember it being this hard. When I thought back to my life with my shopping cart, the world had had rounder edges. Now I was stuck between two worlds: the using one and the "normal" one. I had a job, true, but it was based on my experience as an addict. And yes, I had a place to live, but it was a few feet away from people smoking crack in the doorway. I looked like every other person, except I had six years of living on and off the streets of San

Francisco to remind me that I was a degenerate dope fiend. This reality was never farther away than the collapsed veins on my arms that reminded me daily that I was different. The pain seemed to never end.

I could not cry at the death of friends.
I could not cry at the shame of my past.
I could not cry at the scars on my body.
I could not cry at the loss of my youth.

But when I momentarily lost my dream, I did cry. I had carried my pain for so long. I was ready to give myself a rest. On my way home that night, I was crying for all the things I had not cried about. It felt good. When I finally got to the door of my building, I was finishing with my intermittent sobbing. I could accept the full range of my feelings again. It took me just a few steps up the stairs toward my room to snap back to reality. This was just a setback. It wasn't going to stop me.

The next day, I was on the phone to any person who would listen to me. Someone suggested I contact an ex-offender program located on the university campus, where there were volunteers who helped people who'd been in jail or prison get into school. Within a few days, I was in their office writing a personal statement about why I should be admitted to the university.

My name is Tracey Helton. Once, I was a promising student. I had a bright future. I could have been a lawyer or a doctor. Instead, I became a drug addict. Addiction hit me so quickly, there

was no one in my life that could explain what
was wrong with me. Opiates took hold of me
the first time I used them. The rest of my life be-
came a long, downward spiral that led to over-
doses, one suicide attempt, and homelessness.

I paused. Yet again, I was explaining to strangers why they should give me a second chance.

Within a week, I got an unexpected phone call. Was I able to start school immediately? The ex-offenders program had convinced the school to create an exception for me. So much had changed in such a short period of time. I cried again that night. I was finally able to allow myself to cry after not being able to in the entire nine months of my recovery. I realized I needed a little more time to work on myself before filling all my free time with more activities. I needed to find someone like a therapist to talk to about all the things I had been stuffing inside myself. I made arrangements to start classes part time in August later that year instead of right away.

When I finally returned to campus for my first day of classes, it was a warm summer evening. I had left my place a little early because I knew how crowded the train out to the campus could be. I stopped at the coffee shop and got myself a chai tea and a snack. I was not going to be caught unprepared this time: All of the food places in the Tenderloin would be closed by the time I would leave class at 10:00 PM. The liquor stores would still be open, their doorways lighting up the blackness, inviting me to come inside. Time and time again I would refuse to give them a second glance.

I finally found my classroom. It was hot, and the windows were open to let in some of the cool sea air. The school was just two miles from the ocean—a world away from the place I called home. I pulled out my notebook—I had bought a few from the school bookstore—and pulled out my special pen, the Dr. Grip. I wrote my name in my notebook: Tracey Helton. I couldn't help but smile to myself. Here I was, back in the classroom. No one was doing this for me. I was doing this for myself. I was older than the other students. I was also much wiser. A twenty-something pulled into the chair next to me, smelling like the winos I had passed at the train station. He nodded his head to give me a "What's up," but I already knew. I had been there. I had been that person. Now, I was just Tracey Helton. I was a student like everyone else. I was not the sum of my past, nor was I broken by it. I had a new self. I was unstoppable.

Chapter 7

FROM MR. RIGHT NOW TO MR. RIGHT

I would never describe myself as a woman who dreams of great romance. I never fantasized about a white knight sweeping me off my feet. Growing up in suburban Ohio, I assumed I could instead ensnare him with my smarts instead of the looks I didn't think I had. Fortunately for him, I never got the opportunity. My lifetime of insecurities and lack of boundaries would have made for an ugly coupling. He may have started out valiant, but no doubt he would have run away as angry and confused as I was for many years.

Nevertheless, after I became sober a white knight did briefly come into my life. And like the legend, he swept me off my feet.

I was living in my little room when I met him. I had received my six-month key tag to mark my clean time a few months earlier. I wore it clipped to my belt as if to ward off evil spirits. I was still in my gender-neutral fashion phase, still was not settled into the fact that I was free to be a woman again, not a sexless creature who hid her true self to avoid violence. I would wear baggy jeans, a loose man's shirt, colorful shoes, and rings on every finger. Jewelry is currency because you can always take it off and trade it for a hit. Although I was 100 percent dedicated to my recovery, old habits were tough to break. I still slept with a sweatshirt over my eyes as when I was homeless; I still pressed my clothes by putting them under my mattress to get sharp creases, as I had in jail; and I still wondered about the value of various items in the street economy. When the dentist asked me what kind of crown I wanted for my tooth, I requested gold. I joked with the dentist, "If I ever relapse, I can get a set of pliers and pull it out." I'm not sure he appreciated the humor. I was well on the road to social acceptability, but I still enjoyed a bit of self-deprecating humor. To add to my improving dental situation, I had finally gotten some contacts, fancy hair products, and a little bit of makeup.

I was feeling unusually self-confident that Thursday night when I walked into the basement of the homeless shelter. I was really trying: branching out, doing different meetings, getting phone numbers from people. The meeting was mostly made up of residents who lived upstairs. The exposed bricks and glass blocks that led directly to the sidewalk up above made the room an icebox. I curled my hands around my coffee for dear life. My sponsor was the secre-

tary every other week. I missed her that night. I was waiting for the meeting to start when the door opened and this
glowing creature backlit in a halo of afternoon light walked
in. He was wearing white from head to toe, his alabaster
tracksuit, leather sneakers, and translucent skin lighting up
the dim room.

I continued to cradle my coffee. I knew this man. Parts
of me were now starting to get warm.

He took a minute to scan the group and then strode into
the room. People parted to let him through, craning their
necks to see where he was going. He walked up to me.

"Man, am I glad to see you, Tracey," he said, embracing
me like we were old friends. I suppose we were in a sense.
We were veterans of the street. We had survived. Travis had
been one of my few crushes. He had seemed like the type
of guy you could depend on, even with a drug habit. I had
been used to men who would blacken my eye over the last
bag of drugs. Travis had never seemed like that. He was
funny, handsome, and able to support himself without a life
of crime.

Now look at us: We were both clean! And damn, he
looked fine, too. My mind was spinning.

I hugged him, convinced the universe had brought us
together. God doesn't make mistakes, we were told in the
meetings. He held on a little longer than an obligatory recovery hug would have required. At that moment I knew we
were on. We made a plan to watch Monday Night Football
in my room. I could not wait to have a real date.

When he came over to my place, I had somehow over-
looked that there was nowhere to sit except for my bed. I

didn't have any other furniture in my tiny space, yet I felt so comfortable with him that I was not embarrassed. It didn't take long before we were catching up on the status of our old friends. They were either still using, in prison, or dead, but instead of it being depressing, we bonded over the fact that against the odds, we had gotten off drugs. He was finishing a yearlong program, reuniting with his son. He was starting his journey as a single parent in recovery. I told him how much I admired his ability to be there for his child when so many children were lost to their parents' addiction.

When he asked to give me a back rub, it didn't feel like a ploy to get me in bed. The whole thing felt natural. I felt like we were meant to be, two damaged souls who managed to find love on the other side. It was like an addict's fairy tale. When he took off my clothes, I did not feel self-conscious about my track marks, which were only slightly healed. My legs, my arms, my thighs, and even the backs of my hands looked like a roadmap to destruction. I couldn't cover up my past. But with Travis, I didn't need to. The track marks were battle wounds. His disregard of them only enhanced my feeling that we belonged together.

What proceeded was something akin to the sexual Olympics. Like Prince Charming, he really did sweep me off my feet, as well as bend me and move me all around. I felt such a strong attraction to him that I felt totally uninhibited, so much so that I managed to pull the muscles in my thighs. I could barely navigate the next day, or the next, or the next. I thought about how it would make him laugh when I told him about my strange gait. I waited for him to call. We had this incredible night—now what?

I began obsessing about his silence. Why didn't he call me? I picked up the phone to make sure it was on the hook. I paged myself to make sure my pager was working. I called his work and hung up the phone. I was so fucking hurt and frustrated. I thought we had this incredible connection. For the next five days, when my legs were still sore, I went to bed after work feeling as I had felt after I started a run on heroin—tired, used, and angry at myself.

After it became clear he wasn't going to call for a second date, I had to hit the pause button. This "rejection," which in reality was nothing more than casual sex and instant gratification, was tempting me to use again. I knew I was not ready for any kind of relationship despite my body telling me otherwise.

People who claim opiates enhance their sexual experience have not been using very long. Once you start using regularly, sex becomes like a unicorn. It may exist somewhere, but you are not seeing it. Many men become impotent, and even if they can get an erection, they can't finish the job. I lived with a man for six months while I was using. We never had sex, not once. We tried with mixed results and I was content not to push the issue. I had no desire. When you have heroin, sex is secondary to the feeling of the drug. Heroin is the sex. Everything else takes a back seat to that feeling.

In the first few days to a month in recovery, guess what comes alive? Some men have an orgasm without even touching themselves. I was chastised in jail for having my hands down my pants when I was supposed to be getting my meal tray in the detox unit. I couldn't help myself. The feeling can be overwhelming, even painful. So is it any surprise that the first thing a heroin addict in early recovery does is search for sex? Why not? It feels good and has immediate rewards. Thus, with a brain full of guilt and shame and a body full of hormones, we go off looking for pleasure, if not love.

I had no model of what a good relationship looks like. As a teenager I was extremely interested in boys, and catalogued their comings and goings in great detail in journals. I had different symbols for boys who were nice to me, who said hello or even just acknowledged my existence. If someone had been interested in me then, I would have jumped in bed with absolutely no boundaries, which of course was what happened when I got older. I told more than one lover, "I don't need you to tell me the truth. I just need you to love me." I would rather be lost in the illusion with someone who barely loved me than be alone. Unfortunately, reality always intruded. Men broke into my life as they did into cars, smashing the window, taking what they could get, and leaving shattered pieces. One man kicked down the door into my life—literally. I had gotten a hotel room, and after two days of dating he kicked in the door when I refused to open it. I had seen all the red flags, yet waved my white one in surrender. I gave up on trying to resist him in a vain attempt to be happy.

I had even dated women a few times. The pattern was the same as with the men. They used me, I used them, or we both used each other. My forms of communication included yelling, crying, and leaving. I never knew how to resolve a conflict. I never learned how to be accountable for my part. In many ways, I was replaying the dynamic I had witnessed in the relationship between my parents. In the early stages, I was just like my mother in relationships. I was overly trusting. I was supportive without question. I would also be unable to express my true emotions out of fear that this person would leave me. In the later days of my active addiction, I resembled my father in any relationship. I was the charismatic hustler who was frequently emotionally unavailable. While he had worked long hours most of my life, I ended up working 24/7 to support a drug habit. The parallels made me sick to my stomach.

My addiction was an extremely poor learning lab for my relationships. Love and sex were two totally separate entities in my world. Sex was about a power differential. Love was a weapon used to hurt me. I was trying to come to terms with what sex would mean in my sober life. The feelings that went along with it flooded me and overloaded my systems.

After my encounter with the white knight, I forced myself to stop to take stock. My life had been an endless cycle of searching for the next thing to make me feel okay. Men were just the next logical fix now that drugs were removed. Getting to know a person and being friends was the piece that had always been missing in my relationships. Just as I had with the man who kicked in the door, I would have sex first and then get to know someone after we were already "in a relationship." In truth, love was just another drug to me. It was something to get me outside of myself. If I focused on the other person, I did not have to focus on my problems.

Dating, in or out of recovery, is an awkward dance filled with frequent crushing disappointments. The entire exercise is so completely random. There are six billion people out there. Isn't finding the right one like finding a needle in a haystack? Or in my case, like finding a clean syringe at the trap house? At first, I thought there was no way I could ever date a person who was not in recovery. It seemed impossible that a person who had never gone through some of the things I had could ever connect with me. As I got deeper into the dating process, I saw that dating in the "rooms" of twelve-step could be an exercise in embarrassment. This one slept with that one, that one slept with this one. Then the soap opera was in full display as people sipped their coffee while whispering gossip to their neighbor. I admit, I participated as well. Then I began to hear a crude expression ring over and over in my mind: "Don't shit where you eat." During my dating adventures, it got harder and harder to sit in the same recovery rooms with men I was thinking about dating. How could a person be honest about her secrets when she was trying desperately to impress someone across the same room? I began to realize that, to truly change my life, I would need to let go of some old patterns. I would have to be willing to try to step outside my usual pattern of reaching for the closest thing that made me feel better. Eventually, I would have to step out into the unknown.

I decided to set up some guidelines for myself, some criteria. The first: no kissing and no sex until I got to know a person. This rule quickly weeded out men who were just interested in getting in my pants. The first guy I met told me he supported my recovery, but when I set limits he quickly lost interest. The second one had that neediness that drew me right in. It soon became clear he needed a counselor, not a girlfriend. I found it easy to break things off with him since nothing had really started. Was there a lesson there? The next man said he was just interested in spending time with me, no sex. I was almost offended until he disclosed that he thought he was gay, which he had suppressed with a decade of heroin use. I then met a man who gave me an uncomfortable vibe. It wasn't that there was something wrong with him. I just got the strong feeling he wasn't right for ME. In the past I would have hung in there just because he was so nice to me. This time, I followed my gut to stay away. It was hard, but I knew I was making the right choice. Another man I avoided put his next girlfriend in the hospital a few months later. I could feel myself changing incrementally. I was learning healthy ways of navigating the world of dating.

A friend of mine told me she wanted me to meet someone. I was open to it, thinking that maybe I'd have better luck if a girlfriend did the pre-screening. Out of millions of potential partners, I had become a deadbeat magnet, attracting men who had no job, no prospects, and often a chip on their shoulder. Because so many dates ended with me at home alone watching crime shows, I had no expectations when I met Christian with a group of friends outside a pizza place in a touristy area of San Francisco.

By this point I had slowly acquired a small, dependable circle of friends both in and out of meetings. I was no longer constantly afraid to go places by myself for fear that I would end up using drugs. I was still cautious, but I was learning that I could actually enjoy my life.

My caution about going out was not completely unfounded. Despite whatever progress I had made, I was still living in the Tenderloin, surrounded by the markers of my former life. To make myself feel safe, I had to have every detail of an evening planned out. How was I getting home? What time? Would these people wait for me to get in? More than one evening, I had come home late and been locked outside while the doorman completed his rounds of the building. Being locked out a few blocks from the open-air drug market at two in the morning was scary even for someone without my background. I was used to the day-to-day interactions, but late night was not a time for me to be on the street. Despite my newfound confidence, deep inside I was terrified that if I went out at night without a solid plan, temptation would kick in and I would wind up using. Over and over again I had seen residents from my building get sucked back into the mix outside. I didn't want to be one of those people.

Fear had been my constant companion for so long, the company of friends was a joyous event when I eventually did go out. After being invited out by people in recovery a few times, I finally was able to briefly cast my fear aside and accept an invitation. I had met these friends through a mutual interest in seeing local bands. They were a mixture of people who did not drink at all and those who did but never seemed to drink in front of me, putting me at ease. Christian was one of those people. Right away, I knew he was different from most of the men I had met in my life. Tall and blond, he had boyish looks. He broke all my relationship stereotypes. For one, he was not tattooed as if he had stepped off the prison yard. He looked unused and untainted by life's hardships.

I didn't know many people in our group, and Christian tried to make me feel a part of the conversation. When I talked, he stopped to listen.

Someone told a funny story about some crazy people at her job. I nodded in agreement and someone asked me, "Are they crazy at your work too?"

Without thinking I said, "No kidding, I work with drug addicts like I used to be." I had accidentally outed myself, something I told myself I wouldn't do.

Christian saw my face flush. "Awesome," he said, with such positivity and conviction that it paved over any awkwardness.

And that was that. No stumbling, no questions, no stigma surrounding my past. It was out there and everyone moved on. I wanted more of this, I thought. I don't remember if Christian shook my hand when we met but I know he gave me a big hug goodbye.

When I was invited to join the same group to go to a club, I jumped at the opportunity because I hoped Christian would be there, and it was in a different part of town but close enough for me to walk home safely, avoiding the hustle and bustle of the drug market. My philosophy was, if something was triggering cravings, I would immediately leave that place. My recovery was more important than anyone's hurt feelings over my departure. The most critical thing to me was keeping a needle out of my neck.

When I got to the club it was crowded; the venue was hosting a marathon of bands. We could be there for hours. Christian saw me looking around for a place to sit and with a shy smile said, "You can sit here." He patted his knee.

I was self-conscious of the weight I'd gained since getting off heroin. I almost refused his offer. "Aren't you afraid I'll hurt you?" I said with feigned nonchalance.

He gave me a gentle smile. How could I refuse? As I moved to sit down, he slowly put his arm around me and drew me in. With his embrace I experienced a feeling so strange to me. I felt not only secure but also invited. For the first time I felt like a puzzle piece that fit without the aid of drugs.

The next day Christian didn't call. How many times had I convinced myself that a guy really cared only to find out differently? Here I was, nearly thirty years old, and I had never been in a healthy romantic relationship. Not one. While jumping in and out of station wagons, turning tricks with men with wedding rings and car seats in the back, I had given up any illusion that real love existed. In truth, my main relationship had been with heroin. The drug was a huge part of my life for so many years, consuming my energy as no person could. But I had moved on. I felt ready to open up to the possibility that I was wrong about love. Could it really exist? I had to have faith it would come to me when I was ready for it. I was willing to put my trust in the universe. I could navigate my life with faith instead of constant doubt. I decided not to spend my week chained to the phone waiting for it to ring. He was much younger. I wouldn't take it personally if he never called.

When Christian eventually called, we talked on the phone for two hours. It was like high school should have been. Our conversation was easy; there were no awkward gaps, no silences. At this point in my life, I suffered from what I call ODD, over-disclosure disorder. I figured it was easier to tell someone everything right away to protect myself from rejection. Better to put it out there up front. Christian listened to me ramble about the gory details of my past without judgment.

Finally I ran out of steam.

"Are you done?" he asked. I was taken aback by this. Had I said too much? Was I scaring him away?

He sensed my confusion and said, "You seem like you have a lot to say. I just want to make sure you got it all out."

We agreed to go see the movie *Gladiator* the day before my thirtieth birthday. When we got to the theater, I felt nervous and expectant. My dress was as tight as my shoes. I surprised myself. I could speak in front of a room of one hundred people and talk about being a junkie, yet when I was walking with him, the butterflies in my stomach made me practically forget my name. This was new. I loved it. We held hands in the dark theater, and two hours into the movie, he kissed me.

"Why did you wait so long?" I asked.

"I was working my courage up to it," he said. "Plus I knew how much time I had left."

"How's that?" I said.

"I already saw this movie."

We laughed and I kissed him again. In all my past relationships, I would eventually feel like I was somehow using this person, which made me feel dirty. Not with Christian. I felt I was in unfamiliar territory, but I didn't feel afraid. Instead I felt innocent.

I invited him to come home with me. As we curled up in my single bed in my tiny room at the sober living house,

I realized love was not the drama that it came with during my active addiction. No one needed to scream under my window or follow me for miles to "win me back." Love can be quiet and supportive. I thought I had been in love many times, but I saw now that it was the drugs pulling sick people together. I learned from living on the street to sleep with one eye open. Tonight I clung to the feeling of security as my eyes grew heavy. In that bed, the two of us pressed against each other to keep from falling off. This felt like something worth having. I held on tight.

Chapter 8

I DON'T DESERVE HAPPINESS

"You guys have an empty room?" my friend asked as she toured the apartment.

I nodded. "Yes, but I can't think of anything I want to put in there. I use it as a yoga room."

"A yoga room?" she asked. "Since when do you do yoga? I thought you hated it."

I felt the effects of foot-in-mouth disease. I am well-known for this condition. I had talked so much shit in the past about yoga, but I tend to hate anything new—or at least I think I do.

"In fact," she continued, "you told me it was hippie-dippy bullshit, as I recall."

I swiped my shoulder to indicate I was brushing off her comments. "I am evolving as a person, Mary," I countered. "Besides, it is hippie-dippy bullshit." *I just hope it is hippie-dippy bullshit that actually* works, I think to myself. I had stopped eating meat and quit eating fast food. In terms of self-care, yoga seemed like the next logical step.

I pointed down the hall to guide her toward the living room. As she followed me, I added, "I don't really have anything to put in there anyway. They didn't teach me interior design at Crack High." I was learning that there were so many things a person needed to fill out an apartment. I was never into material possessions, just survival.

We walked toward the back of the apartment. She had a seat on our couch. I hesitated to tell her where it had come from. Nearly all the furniture in the apartment had been the possessions of people who died in assisted living. I was not sure if a person actually died on the couch, but I could picture it. It was so darn comfy, it seemed like as good a place as any. These items were passed on to us when the family passed on claiming them. I could see why. They made me feel strange at times, wondering if Aunt Edna had kept her special newspapers in the same spot in the dresser drawer where I now had my checkbook and my vibrator.

I was ashamed to admit that suburban life made me uncomfortable. I hated to talk to anyone about it, because it made me seem ungrateful. I had hit upon a needle in the San Francisco haystack. I waited, and waited, and waited, and waited some more, until *finally* an opportunity came along to rent the bottom half of a house in one of the nicer areas of the city. Christian and I—living together by now—had a friend who wanted someone he trusted to live below his grandmother. We jumped at the chance, wholly unprepared for the change. For me, it was as if I had been transported to the moon. There were birds chirping, fruit trees in the yard, and a neighborhood cat that needed to be petted upon my arrival home. I was used to rats and roaches, not the pleasant banter of songbirds at 6:00 AM. I was supposed to know something about hanging curtains. I compromised by taking an ugly sheet and nailing it into the walls to cover the window.

This new life could be a real challenge. I had to relearn a laundry list of skills. I had to learn how to cuddle again, to trust having a person sleep next to me night after night. It was hard to stop sleeping with a knife under my pillow. It was also highly unattractive to have jail flashbacks in the middle of brunch. I had to stop devouring my food in less than two minutes or face being ostracized by my companions. I slowly learned to carry a purse. Apparently, an over-thirty-year-old woman reaching into her sweaty bra to pull out money was not socially acceptable with the not-on-drugs set. I also had to stop calling women bitches. "Bitch" is just a term I used when a person was female and I didn't know her name. It wasn't a value judgment to say "that bitch over there" or "Who is that bitch?" Nevertheless, a coworker sat me down to express her displeasure with my description of someone. Finally, I had to learn at work functions that some people can actually drink and enjoy the taste. I had switched jobs around the same time that I switched apartments. I was now working at a free methadone clinic at a hospital. I had been inspired by the passing of Jake. I worked with a mixed crowd of nurses, doctors, social workers, and counselors. At the holiday party, I learned that some people bring a bottle of wine and don't drink it all. Or they may even leave it for the host or hostess. To top it off, not everyone rummages through medicine cabinets. I still believe that holiday party needed to end with a Breathalyzer. We should have brought one in from the clinic—there was plenty of overindulgence that made me feel at home, even if I wasn't the one making a minor fool of myself.

Things between Christian and me had hit a comfortable stride. At five years, this was my longest relationship, healthy or unhealthy, ever. He worked, I worked. We took vacations. We visited his family or my family on major holidays. My mother loved Christian—LOVED, as she would say in exaggerated terms for emphasis. After a rocky start, my father warmed up to him. The first day they met, my father sat right next to Christian on the couch and completely ignored his existence. After a few days, my father saw the light after Christian tolerated both his occasional off-color joke and his excessive drinking. At the airport, he shook Christian's hand and told him, "You are a real asshole, but I like you." That was his attempt at connection. Christian won my heart as he leaned in and joked, "Now I understand why you wanted to leave home." Yes! Finally someone who truly understood me.

It wasn't that I didn't love my parents. They were certainly . . . different from me. In my youth, I had made no effort to understand them. As time went on, I decided to accept them as they were, as they had tried to accept me. The more I took responsibility for my own actions, the less time I spent being critical of others, including my parents. While they would never like my fashion choices or those "damn tattoos" as my mother called them, for the first time in my adult life they respected me. There is a saying, "Would you rather be right or would you rather be happy?" My whole family and I loved to argue when we thought we were right. We also discovered ways to navigate our differences to find a way to be happy with each other.

I was plugging away in graduate school (I had earned my bachelor's degree and started right away on my master's), and still going to twelve-step meetings, although my attendance had decreased over time. In the first five years I would go to meetings three to five days per week. Now, I only tried to make it once a weekend. To try to keep up on all our friendships, we had even started hosting monthly social events at our house, with a mixture of my recovery friends and Christian's bandmates. Life was good for us. But something seemed to be missing. There had to be more to life than school, work, brunch, and nightlife. Our apartment felt empty. Our life felt like it was missing something. We had talked a little about having a child, but it never seemed as if it was the right time.

"There is never a *right* time to have a baby," my mother told me.

I scratched my head as I adjusted the phone. "Well, how will I know, Mom, when I'm ready?"

She laughed. "Well jeez, Tracey. You are already in your mid-thirties." She let an awkward pause hang in the air for emphasis. "How much longer do you think you can wait?"

Her words repeated in my mind. They stung me. Was

my super-conservative mother suggesting I have a baby out of wedlock with my much younger boyfriend? I guess she was . . .

"You aren't getting any younger," she told me with a serious tone.

I was almost offended by this, except I knew she was right. Damn.

Christian and I went on a romantic getaway in Sonoma County. This was our six-year anniversary trip. Our anniversary is the day before my birthday, so we were here to celebrate the two events at one time. We decided on a cozy bed-and-breakfast with a hot tub in our room. The place was slightly janky—much different from the pictures—but I think that made us feel more at home. We brought our dog Sadie, one of our fur children. First there was Smokey the cat, the rescue from a senior citizen in distress. Next came Stephanie the kitten from the SPCA. I had thought Smokey might be lonely. I was wrong. Last came Sadie Girl. She was a rescue from Hurricane Katrina. I was not allowed to get any more animal companions. I loved having that unconditional love in my life, but friends told me they worried that I was going to hit crazy-cat-lady status without an intervention.

It was so nice to get out of the city. The area where I worked was known for the collection of human waste strewn about the doorways. I had discovered this myself one morning as I took Sadie on a long walk to the area. Getting out with her was my stress relief. At that time, I was working full time at the hospital-based methadone clinic, giving out naloxone (which can help reverse an overdose in progress) at a needle exchange, and going to school part time at night. This had been my grind for years. If my schedule wasn't overloaded, it felt empty. Even with the constant obligations, many times I still felt like my life was not headed in the right direction. All this work, yet I was missing a family. I loved my animals, but I felt like it might be time to take the next step. I thought I was incapable of taking care of anyone besides myself, but my furry friends had given me a little more confidence in myself. As the dog curled up next to me, I looked at my pack of birth control pills. Birth control was the only drug I had taken in the past eight years. I had been vigilant.

I had always wanted a child, but it came to feel like an impossibility during my using days. It took many years to get to where I felt stable enough to support myself. Then I found Christian. I was not searching for the love of my life. In the random cosmic joke called dating, I had actually found someone. Finding the right partner was a happy accident. I worried that trying for a baby would tempt fate. I was getting up there in years. Maybe the disappointment would be more than I could handle.

I could see Christian enjoying the breeze flowing into the back of the cabin.

"When we get back to San Francisco I am done with my pills," I announced.

I was saying this to the universe. *I am just going to do it.*

He nodded his head and said, "I told you 'Okay' a year ago." Truth!

When I hit thirty-five, the slow tick of the biological clock became a humming in my ears. At thirty-six, it became a crashing thunder. I had a good job—not great, but perfect for me while I finished graduate school. I had been doing counseling since I was nine months clean, working my way up the ladder into a job with decent benefits and pay. I was not entirely sure this was the "right time," but I didn't know how much time I had left to decide. It seemed as if every magazine I read said something about my expiring eggs. It was pure evil—this decision-making process. How long could a woman wait and reasonably expect to be able to have a child?

About a month after the Sonoma trip, I woke up feeling uneasy. I had been feeling the same way for a few days. I assumed it was normal Monday blues until the feeling dragged into Wednesday. Suddenly I felt so tired, the type of tired that wasn't quelled by a second or third cup of coffee. I couldn't have another anyway. My stomach was queasy. Since the trip, I had diligently scoured the Internet in search of information about how long it would take me to get pregnant. Nevertheless, when I got to work and Googled my symptoms, my heart jumped out of my chest. Could I be pregnant so soon? There was no fucking way this could be possible.

I never got pregnant during my addiction. Not once. This made me skeptical now that I was actually trying. Condoms and drug use do not always go hand in hand. While I'd been good about using condoms with my customers, my boyfriends were another story. More than one tested positive without telling me. HIV had killed most of my friends at a time when there was no medication. My friends were told they were going to die. Unfortunately, this did not stop me from risky behavior. I had to deal with thinking I had HIV more than one time. That seemed to go with the territory. But pregnancy? Never. I was frequently tested at health clinics. I never had a positive test. I barely even had a period. Six months, a year, another eight months of no periods was par for the course.

Strangely, the first person I thought of was my mother. Shouldn't I be thinking of my partner? He couldn't take my call anyway, I told myself. My mind was racing. What would I tell my mother if it was true? What would she think? It was one thing to talk about having a kid. It was an entirely different matter to actually be pregnant. Could she imagine me as a mother? She had seen the worst of me when I had gone home once in the depths of my addiction. It was a week after my brother's wedding. I fucked that whole thing up by showing up back at home for the first time in two or three years a week after the ceremony. I had gotten distracted. I am not sure how I ever made it to the airport. I did a "farewell to San Francisco" hit of speed before I got on the airplane. I was so paranoid the whole flight that I drank booze to take the edge off the voices I was hearing. I arrived at the airport in Kentucky geezed out of my mind. Suddenly I realized I had no idea how I was going to get to West Chester, which was in the next state and forty minutes away. My parents knew I was coming, but both of them were going to be out of town. My father had taken a side job working in a coal mine. My mother was on a long-planned vacation. Getting home was going to take some effort, especially since I had spent the last of my money on drugs and that plane booze.

Somehow, I ended up taking a free hotel shuttle to downtown Cincinnati. Then, tweaking out of my mind, I walked eight miles from downtown to a place where I could catch a bus toward the suburbs. I walked through all the worst areas of my former home city. I saw the old buildings that look like burned-out bomb shelters, a methadone clinic, and a pharmacy of known ill repute that would sell you codeine cough syrup without a prescription. I passed by all sorts of dead-end alleys and housing projects with gated exits. Many of my friends had gotten lost in there. It seemed like they would never make it out. San Francisco was my personal mousetrap. It was amazing that I had extracted myself to come on this trip.

At a gas station, I hitchhiked the rest of the way to my parents' house, far from the city. Their street was dark, and the only night creatures I saw were animals, not people. But when I got to the house, I nearly peed my pants when I saw the shadow people waiting for me on the back porch. Meth has a unique set of bugaboos that come on after sleep deprivation sets in. I would see mystery people out of the corner of my eye. Only this time, it wasn't a shadow. My mother had a life-sized cutout of Billy Ray Cyrus of "Achey Breaky Heart" fame on the back porch. His mullet drove me from the house. I was so uncomfortable that I turned around and walked a mile to the gas station to get a Dr. Pepper. When I got up the courage, I made my way back, went inside, and fell into my old bed. I felt like a child again, with very adult problems.

After a few days alone bouncing off the walls in the house by myself, my mother returned from her vacation. I am quite sure she was shocked by my appearance. I had a chipped front tooth, I was weathered from the sun. She came up to my old room and brought me some food as if I was ten years old and home sick from school. I was so nervous, within a few minutes of small talk I blurted out the truth.

"Mom," I told her, "I am a bisexual junkie prostitute in San Francisco and if you can't accept me, I am going to hop the first freight train home."

In her best '70s-TV mom voice she told me, "I think you need some rest."

She slowly closed the door. There was nothing else to say.

Because of that trip, she could no longer deny the truth. It was right in front of her. Within a week, she was driving me to the clinic to get an HIV test because I had contracted thrush, which was on the short list of illnesses associated with HIV. We waited a week to find out I was negative. She tried to get me to stay in Ohio, but I wasn't ready to stop using drugs. As she kissed me goodbye a month later, she could never have imagined it would be years before she would see me again. At least when I returned again, I was nine months clean. Now, I might be pregnant around the age when she had first become a grandmother. I needed to get some answers before I talked to her.

The next day, I was at work alone at a satellite site. No one else had arrived. It was 6:30 AM and still dark outside. I wanted to talk to someone. I felt different. Something was different about me. During my break, I walked nervously past the resident crackhead to the corner drugstore to get a pregnancy test. I did urine testing as part of my job, yet I fumbled with the test. I got pee all over my hands. As I dried my hands nervously with a paper towel, a matching pink line slowly appeared on the test. My mind had trouble comprehending what that meant. I hadn't bothered to read the directions.

"I don't believe it," I whispered aloud as if someone could hear me.

I tried to regain my composure enough to get my pants up, wash my hands, and walk to go find my coworker, who I knew would be in the office by now.

She took a brief glance as I shoved the test into her workspace.

In her best nurse voice she told me, "Yup. You are pregnant."

Those words were the sweetest ever spoken to me, validating like nothing else. My coworker, the stoic nurse, was also in recovery. She knew what this moment meant for me. I was over the fucking moon.

When I saw my baby's lovely heartbeat on an ultrasound screen a few months later, it was as if the past was erased and everything in my life was focused on that moment.

"Christian," I said as he held my hand, "that is our baby!"

I saw this man I love in a whole new way. It wasn't but a few days later when he dropped to one knee and asked if I would marry him. There was no ring, no date, just a promise of our own little family. Everything was falling into a beautiful place.

When I told my mother about my pregnancy, she was happy. Not just for me, but for herself. She told me she preferred being a grandmother over motherhood in many ways. When the kids were fussy, she explained, she could always hand them back. Over time, my mother had become my best friend. I called her every Sunday, as I did in my addiction, but on these calls I did not ask her for things. In my youth I'd never been able to communicate my feelings to her. She had that motherly disapproval that drove me crazy. Now, she was proud of me. Despite her fears of flying, she had traveled all the way to San Francisco for my college graduation. She said she had not been on a plane in probably forty years. Seeing the look on her face when I handed her my diploma was one of the happiest moments of my life. I had always been so selfish, so focused on the things that I wanted for myself. I never cared about the impact it had on her. I just assumed she would always be there for me. Now, as I matured, I realized that the relationship with my mother was a gift. She had always loved me, even when I could not love myself. Now, with my pregnancy, I could connect with my mother as a woman for the first time. I had a vision of things to come; my suffering now had meaning. It would manifest as the gift of wisdom that I would give my beautiful baby. *If only I can be half the woman, half the mother, she was to me*, I thought to myself as I rubbed my belly.

But my vision ended in perhaps the worst thing to happen to me in my recovery. I was at work when I started to bleed. Red blood in the toilet. *I am fucking dying*, I told myself. Never, for one second, had I ever considered the idea that I would have a miscarriage. This pregnancy had happened so quickly. Surely, it was meant to be! I was in shock. A male coworker who had known me for years took me to the hospital. In the fifteen-minute ride to the emergency room, he tried to assure me that things would be all right. I was grateful he never tried to tell me the baby would survive. Instead, he reminded me that I was a strong person, that I had overcome many trials in my life. He helped me out of the car as if to remind me that someone cared for me.

I entered the hospital in a panic, only to be told to have a seat. I had no pain, no cramps, just blood. I told them I had just seen the baby's heartbeat a few weeks ago. My baby was alive! I couldn't help repeating this to medical professionals as if to counter what I knew was coming. I had to repeat my age, my weight, my addiction history, and my condition over and over in painful detail. With every disclosure I felt my heart sinking into my body. *I am a fucking junkie and God doesn't believe I deserve a baby*. How could I have fooled myself into believing otherwise? Look at my history: eight years of heavy drug use. Is this someone who deserves a baby? My shirt was covered in tears.

I didn't have a cell phone, nor did my fiancé. The process at the hospital dragged on for hours. I had hours to cry on a cold examination table while my dream of a family slipped away from me. Waiting was the hardest part. I had to prepare myself for what I already suspected. It was confirmed on the ultrasound. The technician was not supposed to tell me, but I forced him to as he continued his search for a heartbeat by waving the wand back and forth over my abdomen.

He told me softly, "I should have found a heartbeat by now."

"I saw it two weeks ago," I repeated.

I noticed how the baby had grown from the last appointment. My baby was still in there!

"The doctor will come talk with you . . ." he trailed off as he walked out of the room.

He had been instructed not to talk to women like me. He'd been told not to give us answers. He was to speak in vague terms and let the doctor play the role of the hero or the villain.

After an hour the doctor emerged from behind the curtain. According to my urine test, my pregnancy hormones had evaporated like my hopes.

"This sometimes happens with a first pregnancy," the doctor told me in a sympathetic tone.

This didn't help me. Nothing could help me now. I had lost my baby. I had sucked too many dicks. God was punishing me for all my poor choices. I knew it.

They reviewed my options. I could go the natural route, waiting to expel the "tissue" (no one uses the word "baby"). I could take a pill that would finish the process at home. Both of these presented the risk of blood clots or not fully expelling the "tissue." Or, I could get a "procedure." The D&C was going to require some sedation, but the chances were good they could get all the "tissue" the first time. I wanted to throw up. I went from looking at onesies to selecting how to complete the end of my pregnancy in less than twelve hours. I opted for the procedure. I couldn't bear the thought of having this drag on for weeks.

"We're going to give you some meds in an IV," the nurse told me.

I immediately asked, "What kind of meds?" It started with drugs. It ended with drugs. My life was fucked by drugs.

They explained that they were going to give me a cocktail of benzos to help me "relax," just like the kind I used to take by the handful. I couldn't refuse, I didn't want to refuse. I didn't want this to be happening. I felt so powerless.

Christian arrived as they were about to wheel me into the operating room. They took off my engagement ring. It used to be my mother's—she had given it to me years ago when she finally believed I could stay off drugs. I finally had a reason to wear it. I was going to be married! Now, I was a washed-up old whore who couldn't even carry a baby.

Before they put me under, I told my nurse I was an addict. He poked around my arms looking for a vein.

"Those veins are gone," I assured him.

He pulled my arm up to search the other side. Suddenly my mind clued in that they were going to inject me with drugs. I had not even taken a pain pill when I had a tooth extracted! Now, they were about to shoot me up. Just like old times. For that split second, I was in that old familiar place of searching for a vein. I was anticipating the deliciousness of drugs. Then I remembered why I was here: my baby. When the needle slipped into my skin, I felt the sting. What stung more was the fact that I really wanted to get high for the first time in many years. The loss of my baby was too much to bear. I had never been in this place before, and it was ugly. I needed to ask for help.

I begged the nurse, "Please tell them I am in recovery."

He told me to relax as I felt the drugs go in. That was the last thing I remember for a few hours. When I snapped out of my drug haze, it was time to go home. I was shaky as I heard them explaining the post-operative instructions to Christian.

"Thirty Vicodin," I heard from the doctor.

"No. I can't," I whispered to Christian.

They were about to send me home from the hospital with thirty pills. I wanted to die, and they were giving me the means to kill myself. In fact, I wished I had died. I was so fucking sad. I told myself these feelings would pass. *If I take all those Vicodin*, I thought, *it will set off a dark place, and I may never recover*. I needed something for my pain, but I knew drugs were not the answer.

We came up with a plan. Someone else would hold the medicine for me. I would get a script for ten pills and call if I needed more for the pain. I was not a martyr. If I needed medication, I would take it. But I was also not going to set myself up for failure.

I made more plans. A day or two later, I was back on the Internet, Googling how long I needed to wait before we could try for another baby. I was obsessed with this thing that had been so elusive. I had succeeded in every other thing I had tried to do in recovery. Was I being punished for the sins of my past? Was I not worthy of a child? The fears and inadequacies began to eat me alive.

The worst part was that in my exuberance I had been foolish enough to tell people I was pregnant. Now I would have to explain to all of them that I had lost the baby— though "lost" was not the right term. I did not lose the baby. The baby died inside of me. I was not a worthy host. I was angry and bitter. On top of that, I had pain medicine.

When I was a depressed young adult, drugs provided me with a means of survival. They numbed my emotions so I could make it through the day. The drugs had worked at one point in my life. That time was over. There was no situation in my life that would be improved by drinking or using drugs. I knew that now. The prescribed medications complicated my situation, but not my goals.

I had to stay clean.

When people say they will never get clean, I tell them "never" is a strong word. Instead of saying, "I will never get clean," why not say, "I will stop using drugs one day, but today is not that day." It's better to leave yourself room for the possibility that things will be different tomorrow from how they are today.

In the middle of those tough weeks after my miscarriage when I was struggling to make it to the next moment, I constructed a similar story for myself. Yes, there was laundry. Yes, there were dirty dishes. Yes, I forgot to feed the animals. I was simply doing the best I could in a difficult situation. Instead of berating myself, instead of thinking in absolutes, I re-framed my thinking and poured my grief into action. I learned about my body. I learned about steps I could take to increase my chances of pregnancy. I did not let the pain push me back into active addiction. Instead, I channeled it. I was a woman with a mission. If there was one thing I knew about myself, it was that I am determined. I would find a way . . . one more time.

Chapter 9

CRISIS

When the epilogue of my life is written, no one will ever be able to say that I wasn't determined. One night I was sucking down a carton of saag paneer and rice. The only thing to come out of having a miscarriage that is not completely horrible was being able to eat sushi and spicy food again. Indian food numbed my mouth and my pain. I knew I would regret all this garlic and spice tomorrow. Tonight I was in the mood to say "Fuck it." There was a place close to my house that delivered. The proximity of that place and my mood made for a perfect storm of indulgence and isolation. Despite pleading from my fiancé, I couldn't bear to leave the house when I was not at work or school. Everywhere I went, it seemed like I ran into someone who wanted to discuss the progress of my now-lost pregnancy. Since I'd been stuffing my feelings with food, I could see where I would still look pregnant. But I was sick of explaining myself: I am no longer "with child." Now I just look, feel, and eat like I am fat. I was oh-so-bitter. One day I might take a few steps forward, the next it was a few steps back.

I had to be out of work for a few days to heal. Plus there were the pain meds. Seeing me with pinned eyes certainly would not be inspiring to the methadone patients seeking my assistance. I felt like I was having the worst period in the history of womankind. I was having cramps. I was tearful. I wanted to eat everything. Eating was my way of dealing with depression. The food gave me a way to shove down the feelings. I was still trying to process the shock of the event. I had felt so powerless lying there on the gurney as they wheeled me through the halls. I had felt so empty at home knowing there would be no "special delivery" on March 31. My friends wanted me to talk, but I didn't know the words to describe the pain I was feeling. I just wanted to pass the time without feeling anymore. I spent hours researching the nuts and bolts of getting pregnant using an ovulation tracker. With a click of the mouse, I transported myself to a new fantasyland where having a baby would be possible again. The fantasy allowed me to block out my painful reality. It was not just the loss of the child that threw me into a state of despair. I had an utter loss of hope. The world seemed as cruel as it had before I had quit drugs. I had fallen into the trap of believing that I could be a "normal" person. I had started to believe that I would be able to have a family, to have a house filled with love, unlike the one I'd had as a child. The loss of the child was the death of my dreams.

Before the pregnancy I was going to meetings sparingly because of my heavy course load at school. I found that getting to one meeting a week could be a struggle. Now my attendance had been even more sporadic. I found it difficult to hear a room full of mostly men explain all the things their "higher power" had done for them, when I felt like he, she, or it had let my baby die. I really began to notice the gender disparities in those meetings. It seemed as if there were at least five men for every woman. In the past, I had been going to the one women's meeting every week in my area, but I could no longer fit it into my schedule. My miscarriage also wasn't a topic I felt I really wanted to share at a group level. Instead I was sitting in my dark bedroom, clicking away, hoping that somehow I could find an answer to my spiritual crisis.

I was trapped in my own thoughts, with the healthy exception of calls here and there from concerned friends. But it was still too hard to talk to anyone who knew me. They tried, they really tried, to help me. But I just felt as if there was no one who understood the depths of my pain. Miscarriages, though very common, seemed to me to be taboo. The lack of information or discussion about them made me feel like a failure as a woman. I was so inept, I couldn't even carry a baby to full term.

When I took to the magic of technology to find out how long I needed to wait in between pregnancies, I also found support from strangers. On the Internet, I felt I could share my pain without judgment. There was a whole community of women who had experienced the same thing. Those women found solace from behind their avatars. I had nothing fancy to offer. I created traceyh415. That would be my new Internet identity.

"How are you ladies tonight?" asked babyfever1970.

"I am okay," I typed. "Finally stopped crying."

"Don't worry," added AngelWings2006, "we understand. Let it out."

"(((HUGS)))" said sugarbearinTX. There were sparkles in her avatar. I suddenly loved sparkles.

Somehow, I felt this hug. For a split second, I felt a tiny bit better.

I was asking anyone who would listen about my chances of getting pregnant again—nurses, doctors, and counselors. I got a lot of "I can't answer that question." I suppose that was normal since they worked at the methadone clinic, not in the field of reproductive technology. But that didn't deter me from asking. I was a professional. I had a degree. How could there be no possible way I could take control of this situation? The loss of control was sending me spinning like a top on the ledge of a skyscraper. I was thirty-six years old! I could not wait much longer.

In a moment of complete desperation, I made an appointment with a fertility clinic. Even my fiancé gave me the "I am going along with this, but are you fucking crazy?" eye roll. I paid $350 for a doctor to tell me the equivalent of Your eggs are fine, chill out. I went from heroin addict to baby addict. Is that even a thing? I wondered to myself. If not, I have invented a new addiction.

This obsession was slowly starting to take over my life. All I could think about was how horrible my life would be if I could never have a child. Why was I so stupid? Why did I believe all that garbage I had seen in women's magazines telling me I could have the family *and* the career? Why did I wait so long? It all seemed like such bullshit now. I just wanted to have someone call me "Mommy." I wanted to know I would never be alone again. I wanted to have that feeling of being part of a family, *my* little family. I was incurable. I felt a little saner when I immersed myself in my plan. I constantly practiced my new language: cervical mucus, ovulation tables, luteal phases, and basal body temperatures. It was as if the pursuit of a baby was the only thing that could help me manage the pain over the one I had lost. I knew I was running from my feelings. I was running the way I ran with drugs. I was going to drive this car until the wheels fell off.

"Let your body heal," the ob-gyn told me.

I was in his office for my follow-up appointment, six weeks after my procedure.

"Tell me the truth," I asked him, "what is the minimum amount of time I need to wait?"

He helped me down from the table. "I would say three to six months."

His advice fell on deaf ears. I had a case of selective hearing. *Yeah right, three months,* I told myself. *Let's start trying now.* It should be fine since it certainly would take more than three months. I was tuning out all reasonable feedback while filling up my mind with online advice. The women on these message boards hadn't waited! They had perfectly healthy babies! Why not me? I knew I was beyond the point of baby fever. I had baby delirium.

My fiancé was willing to participate in anything that would get me to stop sitting around in the dark in my pajamas. During the "fertile window" of five to eight days, it was required that we have as much sex as humanly possible to catch the egg as it made the journey to my tired old uterus. There was lingerie and porn and lube of all kinds to get the motivation going for the two to three sex sessions *per day* required for this endeavor. By the end of the fertile window, we were sore and tired. Then, we had to wait ten days for the pregnancy tests.

Our impending marriage was completely overshadowed by my obsessions. I was willing to go through with the wedding, but I can't say I was particularly excited about it. Deep down, I felt as if the only reason my fiancé had agreed to marry me was gone. I forced myself to push through my doubts. I got a light purple dress, he got a matching shirt and suit. The idea of wearing white was simply too ironic for me. I felt as if the Christian God, if there is one, would certainly strike me down on the spot. I was fucking with all his traditions. A whore like me didn't need to wear white at my wedding. I certainly was no virgin. I was pure as the snow on the highway. I was pissed at God anyway. This God let my baby die. Fuck him.

I was trying on my off-the-rack dress at home after the alterations when I caught a glimpse of my fiancé in the next room. *Why does he put up with me?* I wondered to myself. This man—I had this man. He loved me. I snapped out of my baby haze to look at this beautiful man. He accepted me for all my crazy. I was trying to squish my size 18 ass into a taffeta dress while he patiently waited for me to come back and watch TV. He thought I was beautiful, and smart, and special. How did I ever manage to get so lucky?

I took another look at myself in the bathroom mirror. I didn't recognize the person I saw there. Here was a woman who was radiant. She was glowing from the inside. Was that me? Was I this person? For a split second, I felt my happiness. It was overwhelming me. It wasn't the marriage or the dress. It was the love we had for each other. WE had been through this horrible thing—together. Every man I had ever cared about had hurt me in some way. Not him, not ever. I got out of my dress and gave Christian a kiss. He deserved much more attention than what I had been giving him the past few weeks. I was going to make a commitment to myself to try harder to be good to him. Within a few days, we were married.

We exchanged vows at City Hall in front of a few friends. It was small and special. I stayed in my dress as we went out for oysters. I exchanged my heels for flip-flops. The first time I wore platform heels in the fifth grade, I had broken my leg. This had been one of a handful of times since then that I had put on heels. It is well documented that I've always had horrible luck with shoes. At least that hadn't changed when everything else in my world was topsy-turvy.

Our honeymoon was an exhausting four days. It certainly was not some wild festival of sexual adventure. We had worn that out in the fertile window. It was exhausting because my young, incredibly fit husband dragged me on hikes from hell around the coast of Kauai. I have never been so tired or sunburned in all my life. Sticking a needle in my neck was as close as I had ever come to testing my adventurous side. Now, I was out inching along the side of wet cliffs while the sun toasted my shoulders well past a crispy red. The next day, to cool off we went swimming on a reef. I got sandwiched between some coral and a hungry sea turtle. My legs got battered by the tide trying to swim away. By the last night, I had collapsed on the couch of our condo. This was just the trip I needed. My husband and I held hands, the only part that was not stinging, as we realized we were in this life together.

A few months later, we found out I was pregnant. I peed on a stick in the bathroom of a Narcotics Anonymous meeting. I was still pissed off at God, but I was trying to get back in to the swing of meetings. I needed the support of my friends there. When I saw that my test was positive, I prepared myself for nine long months of hypervigilance. I would have spent nine months lying on my side on the couch if I knew that would make this happen. Every single cramp or creak sent me into a panic. I ate my way through my anxiety, gaining well over fifty pounds. When I heard that I was eating for two, I took this completely to heart. I think I was actually eating for three or four adults.

Every time I would see the doctor, the result would be the same: high blood pressure. Of course, I was a nervous freaking wreck. I had done all the tests, made every appointment. I would see the doctor and panic would set in. Was something wrong with the baby? Was I ever going to stop gaining weight? Would I ever see my ankles again? So many questions before each visit. I would pull out my *What to Expect When You're Expecting* book to make notes, my tired, swollen legs propped up on the ottoman after a long day at the hospital. The baby swirled around in my belly as she pushed the book up and down. A girl—we were having a girl. The amnio had confirmed it. With the cat on one side and the dog on the other, I would fall into a nap as I daydreamed about what would happen when she was finally here.

I was so worried about the pregnancy, I never gave much thought about the birth. As it got closer to the event, I turned to my mom for advice.

"What happened when you had me?" I asked her. "What was it like?"

I could hear her take a sip of her Diet Pepsi. This was part of her routine since she had quit smoking two packs of cigarettes a day. At night, she would drink diet soda, watch the home shopping network, and hope for the phone to ring.

"Welllllllll." She paused. "I don't remember much."

This puzzled me. I thought this was one of the most important days of her life, the birth of her third baby, the last one. My mother had told me on a few different occasions that she had wanted to have five children. My father was from a large family and my mother was always lonely as an only child. She had some type of bleeding incident after my older brother was born where they advised her not to have any more children. I was born five years later. The day I was born was the day the cicadas started emerging from hibernation, a once-every-seventeen-years event. My mother would joke that my birth was an event of biblical proportions.

"What?" I asked. "You don't remember much?"

She continued, "They knocked me out, Trace. I woke up and they handed me the baby all cleaned up."

I laughed to myself. My mother had presented herself all

my life as this super-straitlaced person. However, it seemed like a wide variety of her parenting stories from the '60s and '70s had involved drugs. She had diet pills to lose the baby weight (stimulants), nerve pills to "deal with the stress of my brother" (benzos), and now I found out she was knocked out during my birth. I guess she didn't see them as being *drugs* since the doctor had given them to her. *It's no wonder I got hooked!* I laughed to myself. Okay, maybe there was my whole picking-up-a-needle thing, too. It was a passing thought.

Her top-notch childbirth advice: Take the drugs. Birth was this natural thing involving some mild sedation. A few pushes—voila! They hand you a baby, you put it in cute clothes, and you live happily ever after with your child. That was the way my mother made it sound. Between her advice and a few episodes of those daytime television shows about childbirth, I felt somewhat prepared. It wasn't until my friend took me to see the movie *Knocked Up* that the reality crept in: One, I was actually going to be having a baby, and two, I had no idea what the fuck I was doing. Mild panic set in.

By thirty-nine weeks, I had really gained *way* too much weight. Apparently, cookies are not a cure for morning sickness, especially when ingested at 2:00 AM when you can't sleep because your stomach feels ripped apart. When you are a fatty and of advanced maternal age, a.k.a. old, every doctor's visit feels like it's about creating fear in the heart of the crazy old lady who dared to fight biology and get *pregnant* rather than read an article on hot flashes from AARP and enjoy her plight as a crone. See? We told you, fatty. You are too friggin' old. Now you have to come in for regular monitoring. Every time without fail, the *thought* of going to the doctor would send my blood pressure through the roof. Between the morning sickness and prenatal testing blues, I couldn't control it.

The doctor shook his head in disapproval.

"Your blood pressure is too high," he told me.

"I hate coming here," I explained. "It makes me nervous."

He pulled the cuff off my arm.

He told me, "If your blood pressure doesn't come down in an hour, we are going to have to induce your labor today."

"Today?!" I choked.

TODAY as in now as in today. What the fuck was happening?!

There would be no laboring at home, no late-night water breaking in my flannel nightgown as I had pictured it. Today was the day! That alone sent my pressure to the ceiling. I was to waddle over to Labor and Delivery immediately.

At this point, I had trouble believing they were going to let me leave the hospital with a baby. The main reason was that every person there seemed to know that I used to be a junkie. And I felt them judging me. I wasn't the mom from the baby catalogue. I was the one with track marks. I was flabbergasted to discover that the process of inducing labor starts with a vein. *Oh LORD,* I thought to myself. Here we fucking go again. Every single staff person in Labor and Delivery that night seemed to find out about me because they could not find a vein.

"Excuse me. Those veins are gone," I told them. "I used to be a drug user."

"Here," they would tell me as they pointed to the next nurse. "Let her try."

This same process was repeated for nearly two hours. Search, poke, quit. Search, poke quit. NEXT! Search, poke, quit. There were people constantly coming in and out of the room. Trying to hide my body during this already mortifying ordeal was impossible. The gown they gave me was open in both the front and the back. I could not tell if the staff here were simply inexperienced or just determined not to listen to me. My frustration was growing with each passing moment.

"It isn't just that we need to get blood out of your veins," they explained. "We need to be able to get fluids *into* them."

That was a new one for me. Of course, I knew absolutely *nothing* about sticking things into my veins. *Should I laugh or cry here?* I thought to myself. I could hear some whispering just beyond my line of sight. It was a discussion about putting a central line in my neck. I blew a mental fuse. How am I supposed to push out a baby with a line in my neck? At this point, I was in angry tears.

GET SOMEONE ELSE IN HERE, I thought. *Now, stat, code blue, or whatever the fuck the term is for it.*

There was a general feeling of concern building among my group at the hospital—my friends, my husband, and of course, myself. This was my first time having a baby. This trip to the hospital was supposed to be the exact opposite of the miscarriage. I was going to be experiencing life. I was getting more and more restless. I felt as if everything was spinning out of control.

Finally, the anesthesiologist came in with an infectious swagger. He tapped me gently on the shoulder as if to say, "I got this." He had that same bravado as the guy in the porn flick who talks about cleaning pipes.

"I heard you were having a few issues, Ms. Helton," he said as he sat down.

I perked up at his confidence. "Yes," I told him, "that is an understatement."

He pulled my left arm toward him. "Just hold still," he asked gently.

In less than five minutes, he had a working line in me. *Here we go.*

The pain started as the Pitocin flowed. I could feel my labor starting. It reminded me of when I had impacted bowel movements while I was on heroin. There was this uncomfortable feeling as if my body was trying to push a boulder out of my lower regions. Soon, there was the offering of refreshments. I would have killed for this easy access to my veins in my prior life. Fentanyl: yes please. My pain score was around a "Fuck yes I would like some more medicine." The epidural going in was as I had expected. Having a needle shoved in my spine was as frightening as anything I had ever experienced up until that point. It made me question my decision not to have natural labor. I couldn't feel the contractions, I couldn't feel the pushing, and I could not feel anything below my chest. Why didn't I go to the childbirth classes? Why did I take the drugs? Why didn't I walk around more? Why did I spend so much time watching *A Baby Story* on television? I believed all the hype. I thought that nature would take some beautiful path and my vagina was a garden that would produce a beautiful flower.

After twenty-five or twenty-six hours, they turned off my epidural.

"We need you to be able to feel when you push," said one perky doctor. Then she ran out of the room.

I hadn't realized so much of my time would be spent with nurses. It seemed as if they did most of the work. It was as if my labor was a television show, and the doctor just came in to do some cameo appearances while getting all the credit.

"FUUUUUUCCCCCCK!" I screamed at the top of my lungs.

My two friends who came for the birth were trying to hold my hand. They were tired and ready to go home. I didn't know what to do except yell, at least partially in their faces. I hurt too much.

The attending nurse asked me, "Do you think you could keep it down?"

"What?!" I asked.

"What?!" my friends asked.

She patted me and told me, "You are frightening the other patients."

After three and a half hours of pushing, I was begging for the C-section. I had heard that childbirth was the number one cause of death for women in the U.S. until fairly recently. I believed it. My baby was stuck. After the birth, a friend of mine told me that the midwives of the past would have had few choices in that circumstance: let me bleed to death or snap the baby's neck. They would pull the baby out, then tell me I could have others. The C-section was actually a relief. The end of the long journey that had started on that vacation to Sonoma County. After thirty hours in labor, three hours of pushing, and one C-section, I was presented with one little screaming red-faced alien I was told was my daughter. The first thing I told my husband after I saw her was, "I want another one." I was in love.

I had watched hours upon hours of shows on various cable channels to learn about what life would be like with an infant. I did not realize I was going to be doing all these things while recovering from major abdominal surgery.

The first thing that surprised me was all the screaming involved in the day-to-day handling of my daughter. I was told by everyone who cared to give me advice that babies have different personalities. I learned within the first few days that her personality involved hysterics—it seemed she cried over every single thing. It was clear by the fourth day that I was the lucky recipient of a pristine baby who would cry the second her diaper got wet or soiled in any way. The nurses tried to calm me down by informing me this would make potty training so much easier later on.

I guess I was having trouble understanding the whole process. I was under the assumption the nurses would whisk the baby away to some special room for a few hours so I could rest. Oh no; I was heartily mistaken. Within forty-five minutes of my surgery, I was being handed my child to feed despite the fact that I had not slept for a few days for more than a few minutes here and there. At one point, I looked over at the baby swaddled next to me.

"Katie," I whispered. "It's your mommy."

I tried to reach closer to the bassinet without pulling the tubes out of my arm.

"It is just me and you now, baby," I told her. Her dad had been sent home by the hospital until they could switch my room.

Katie looked in my general direction with those "I can't really see you" saucer-like newborn eyes. Then, she started to scream her head off. SCREAM.

She screamed bloody murder as I tried to scoot myself over to her.

It would be pretty typical of the first three months with her.

I was discharged from the hospital with a tiny baby, a bag full of painkillers, and a complimentary diaper bag full of paper underwear and pads the length of my arm. My instructions were to not lift anything heavier than the baby. I had been stepped down from one opiate to another, but I knew the pain that would be in store for me when the medicine ran out in a week or two. They explained to me in painstaking detail that I MUST take this medication. If I did not, the consequences could be serious as the pain could impact my healing. My plan was for my husband to manage my pills. I would taper myself off as my pain subsided. I could call if I needed more or dispose of what was left if I needed less.

Baby Kathryn was named after my mother. We called her Katie or Katie-bear. She was so incredibly tiny. They had estimated from her ultrasounds that she would be close to eight pounds when she was born. When we left the hospital, she was less than six. We didn't realize that her weight would fluctuate. Because of the induced birth, my body was not catching up with milk. I felt weird when I was visited on my last day at the hospital by a male lactation special-ist. When he grabbed my boob to show me how to feed the baby, I knew it was time to get the fuck out of the hospital. Things had been too stressful there.

After two weeks of sleepless nights with a baby who wanted to be up every forty-five minutes, I really started to wonder what the fuck I had gotten myself into by having a child. How did I ever think I could take care of another human? There were times I forgot to feed the cats. To add insult to injury, I started having serious withdrawal from the opiate-based medications. I envied women in my online support groups who talked about *finally* being able to have a glass of wine.

On top of tending to my newborn, I was handling the few weeks' worth of work the teachers in my graduate pro-gram gave me to stay caught up. I was up working on my finals projects for graduate school with a runny nose and a baby hanging off my boob. My legs felt like rocks again for the first time in close to a decade. I was having hot flashes and cold chills while trying to do statistical analysis on my final research project. This was my last semester—the cul-mination of nine long years. I had to find a way to push through. If there was ever a time I wanted to curl up in a ball and cry, this was it.

"I think you should go to a meeting," my husband told me. "Get out of the house for a while."

I had to agree with him. "Okay," I agreed. "I can leave the house for a few hours."

I felt as if what he really meant was *he* wanted to leave the house. My husband was sharing feedings, changing all the diapers. He was a fantastic partner. Unfortunately, he was going to have to return to work soon. He wanted to come up for air and so did I. We agreed I would go to a meeting with a friend and the baby while he went to play music for a few hours.

As I pushed Katie in the stroller, my legs felt like they weighed a hundred pounds. The meeting was only ten blocks away, but it felt like miles. While I sat in my chair, I felt as if everyone was looking at me every time the baby made the slightest noise. The room was in the back of a church with acoustics that projected the smallest noise clear across the room. When Katie started stirring, I whipped out my boob and fed her in the meeting. I needed to be there, I needed to stay. When I walked out of that place, I couldn't have told you what the speaker had said, but somehow I felt a tiny bit better. I had passed the first test. I made it out of the house without losing my shit. That was quite an accomplishment.

I put my feet up on the kitchen stool and decided to call my mother.

"When are you coming to visit?" she asked me. She cut out all the small talk. She wanted to see the grandchild she had thought would never happen.

I stroked Katie's hair as she lay on my chest. We'd had a big day. We were both tired.

I assured her, "We're coming right after I finish school, Mom. I just have a few more months."

"Keep those goddamned cats away from her, Tracey," she told me. "They suck away the baby's breath!" I rolled my eyes.

Katie started to whimper a little. I could tell my mom was worried.

"Is that Katie?" she asked. "Put her on the phone."

I put the phone next to her ear.

I could hear my mom. "Hi, Katie. This is your grandma. I love you very much, Katie. I am going to see you very soon. Be good for your mother."

I felt my eyes start to well up with tears. *I am her mother.* My mother tried so hard to be there for me. Just as I would be there for my daughter. Katie doesn't care that I was a junkie. She just wants me to be there for her. I pressed her gently against me. The cycle of life had come full circle for me.

When I got off the phone with my mother, I reflected on how much things had changed. I had tried so hard to kill myself. I had tried to suffocate my emotions. I wanted so much for someone to love me. When that didn't happen, I started poisoning myself. Now, here I was, surrounded by people who loved me. I had my family, my friends, my fur babies, and my precious daughter. I had always seen myself as a victim of the inequities of fortune. Now, my life was completely different. My heart was full of love. For the first time in my thirty-seven years of life, I truly felt loved. I was going to get over this sickness, this funk that had hung over me for so many years. I was going to enjoy this family that was mine. I had searched in a million different places to find something to fix me. The solution was within me the whole time: love. As I closed my eyes with my daughter on my chest I felt a love beyond what I had ever imagined. I was exactly where I needed to be.

Chapter 10

THE BEST PRESENT

"When I die, at least I'll know my children are taken care of," my mother whispered.

Her comment gave me pause. I had one last reservation in my recovery. I was not sure if I could withstand her death without using drugs. I felt that the pain would be unbearable.

I was rocking Katie gently to sleep. Apparently, she had cried the entire time Christian and I had gone out to dinner. My mother had insisted that we have some time alone. I would have been satisfied staying on the couch with my feet up. All this traveling was making me feel swollen. I didn't dare tell my mother yet, but we were going to try for another baby soon. I wanted just to enjoy the few days we had together. Four days visiting my mom wasn't a long trip,

but it was all we could afford. I had no vacation time left.
Since returning from maternity leave, I was barely keeping
my sanity. Between clients, I was either pumping or napping
at my desk.

Katie fell fast asleep in my arms. She was all cried out
after her big night with Grandma.

As I set Katie down to rest, I asked my mom to repeat
herself.

"When I die," she repeated, "at least I know my children are taken care of. Your sister, your brother, you . . ."
her voice trailed off.

"You have a long time left to go, Mom," I reassured her.

I put my arm around her shoulder. My mother seemed
so much smaller now than before. She had a big personality
that filled up a room with her funny stories. She loved to
dance. She loved to scream at the television during the Cincinnati Bengals football games. She loved her country music.
Even when she was resting in her favorite flannel pajamas,
she always seemed to be in motion. Now, she seemed down
to life-sized. I could see her mortality in the way she walked
with her shoulders slightly lowered. She had lost a lot of the
pep in her step.

The last three years of dealing with my father's illnesses
had taken their toll on her. For many years when I was a
young child, I had thought she must somehow be the cause
of his drinking. In my teen years, I was angry because I felt
she was too accepting of his condition. In my twenties, I
gained some humility—I was in no place to judge anyone.
In the years when I was actively using, some would say my
mother "enabled" me. In fact, she probably saved my life.

She found the strength to help me unconditionally in the same way she had helped my father. Our relationship had grown to the point where now I understood their marriage was none of my business. This made my life infinitely easier.

My mother had never talked about her death until recently, as she was getting into her late sixties. She was still trying to convince me to take a cruise for her seventieth birthday. I reluctantly agreed. Our family had started taking destination vacations together around the time I started dating Christian. We created some happy memories together. I was enjoying my family as a unit. As we all had families of our own, our resentments had subsided as our relationships matured.

My mother had always been the glue that held all of us together. Before this trip, she had never seemed to age. A little grayer, some more wrinkles, but basically the same appearance my entire life. She liked Christmas sweaters with brightly matching earrings. She liked to decorate every inch of the house for the Easter Bunny or with pilgrims at Thanksgiving. She always left a lipstick mark on her cup, always had tissues in her purse, and always kept a piece of chocolate stashed somewhere for emergencies.

My father, on the other hand, had been living in a cycle of hospitals, skilled nursing facilities, and residential care homes. His old hospital bed, left over from the period of time when my mother had attempted to care for him at home, was on the back porch. The doctor had told my father directly: He needed to quit booze and quit smoking. These were an impossible task for him. I did see him drink less, but to him beer was a regular beverage, not the gateway to alcoholic despair. I and many of my friends had success in twelve-step, yet my father, despite attending meetings regularly after having a series of strokes in recent years, was never able to achieve lasting sobriety. He was one of those people they describe in the AA literature as being "constitutionally incapable of being honest" with himself. In many ways, I think AA was harm reduction for him. He enjoyed the social element of being with other alcoholics. It helped him drink less and drink in a manner that was less harmful. If only he could have found a program that was more tailored to his goals. I never asked him if he wanted to quit drinking, but his actions told me he did not want to deal with whatever he would be facing without a drink.

After being unable to discontinue alcohol use, my father slowly gained a laundry list of medical conditions that ended in him spending the last of his years partially paralyzed from a stroke and intermittently confined to a bed. I often wondered how it felt for him to have my mother as his caretaker and sole advocate. He had spent so many years complaining about her, yet here she was showing up for him on a daily basis. There was no way to avoid the forty-plus years of history between them. Now, he had to spend every waking moment thinking about how he had fucked up his life by choosing alcohol over his family. It made me see him in a different light. I had done some of the same things he had done. It wasn't that I hadn't loved my family. I just did not know how to stop using drugs. I empathized with his predicament as one I had been in myself. As my father had told me many years before, the only places we addicts end up are recovery, the cemetery, or the penitentiary.

Here on our visit, my mother insisted that we visit him in the nursing home in the morning. The idea of seeing him both sober and fragile was terrifying to me.

My mother had been forced to take a part-time job to cover her expenses. There would be no golden days of retirement for her. Advocating for my father and his medical care had become her obsession as having a baby had become mine. Our lives were so different, yet we could be so similar. Getting me to visit my father was the culmination of her dreams—one chance for our family to be together again.

In the morning, we all stuffed ourselves into the rental van. Signing in at the front desk, I took a deep breath. I wasn't sure what to expect. I hadn't seen my father in a few years.

He was watching Fox News when we entered the common area.

"They are talking about the global warming," he told us. He clicked the remote.

He wasn't much for starting a conversation.

I asked, "How are you, Dad?"

It seemed so strange to call him "Dad." As if we were a normal family.

"I was watching this show talking about that global warming crap," he said. "You know, scientists say that stuff isn't real."

Oh, really! I thought. Please let's start the day with an argument. It will be just like home.

I had barely sat down before my mother snatched Katie from me. She set her firmly on his lap and wrapped his partially paralyzed arm around her. Inside, I was freaking out. I knew he had a catheter and a bag to collect urine. I tried to pull my mother to the side but she wouldn't have it. My daughter was going to sit on his lap whether I liked it or not. I started to feel both small and outnumbered again. This is what she had wanted all along. She knew I would have balked at the visit if I had known the main purpose was to have him hold Katie. I was confused by my lack of compassion. I spent all day with clients asking them to be gentle with themselves, yet it was extremely tough for me to have any sympathy for my father. I felt angry at myself, yet the results were the same. I wanted to get out of there, but I forced myself to stay.

Eventually, as time passed, the conversation became more fluid. There was nothing eventful about the visit itself. It was actually quite ordinary. But there was nothing ordinary about what that visit taught me. After two hours, it was time to leave. I told my father I loved him that day. I think I actually meant it. Sitting there with him, a prisoner of his disease, I finally started to feel an empathy for him that was nearly indescribable. If I had taken one hit more, had just one more infection, just one more needle shoved in my skin, would my fate have been the same? What was it like being so distant from the child who had once worshipped you? What was it like being taken care of by the person whom you had treated so badly? I felt a wave of pain as I touched his hand for the last time. My father started crying uncontrollably. I had no words for what I should say to him. I only knew I gave him one last chance to be in my life. My child had looked up at him as I once had. I had only known my father to cry a handful of times in my life. I was glad it was upon meeting my child and not at my funeral.

In the end, the visit wasn't about me resolving things from the past. There is a recovery saying that when you hold on to a resentment, the only person you are really hurting is yourself. When I first heard this from my seat in the rehab center, it was a revelation. It would have been easy to go on blaming my father for the past. When I let myself go to this place of anger, I frequently felt as if I was causing my own suffering. It was not that I needed to "forgive" my father. I just needed to start from the present tense. I could not change the past. I could only evaluate my life starting with the present. In the moment, I chose to try to get to know him again. I didn't want him to leave this world thinking that I hated him. My gift to him, maybe even to myself, was to acknowledge that I cared for him.

Sometimes I end texts with "I love you," even to people I don't know all that well who are struggling. Because we all need a little more love in the world.

By the time I had worked through my issues by journaling, attending groups, and talking with friends, I realized the ex-boyfriend who told me I was worthless needed an eviction. I had given him too much time and too much space. Bye! This is just one example. Working through my past patterns had allowed me the room in my heart to be prepared for the final trip to see my father.

We receive so many messages about perfection. I do not want to be perfect. I just want to be okay in my own skin. I want to be happy with myself. That is enough. In that moment, in that best present, I chose to let go. I chose to give him what he needed. I told my father that I loved him. Not for me, but for him. I know it made a difference. I didn't forgive him. The visit wasn't about changing the past. I still acknowledged how I felt.

When we left the home, I got the bold idea to make my mother a healthy lunch before we left for the airport. Without anyone to eat with her, the refrigerator had become a graveyard of meals from the past. One thing after another was expired. From meat to cream to condiments. I had the bright idea of making her something I thought was fresh and delicious, a stir-fry with lots of vegetables. I had added healthy cooking to my self-care list a few years back. I wanted her to see how I had evolved as an adult woman capable of taking care of myself and my family. My effort was not well received.

"Tracey," she barked, "you are making a mess."

She started wiping the stovetop.

"I am not even done cooking, Mom!" I told her. "Sit down!"

She kept moving around me as I stirred the sauce.

"Are you going to let me finish?" I asked.

"Well," she told me, "I am not really hungry."

That was the last straw. I put the lid on the pot and turned off the food.

"Let this sit for ten minutes," I told her. "This is done. And so am I."

It was time for us to leave. My mother was starting an argument with me. IT WAS TIME FOR US TO LEAVE. I didn't know when I would make it back here again and she was starting an argument with me over food. I was so frustrated. Why wouldn't she let me help her?

"C'mon, Christian," I yelled to my husband. He finished putting our bags in the car.

Katie smiled as she cruised along the furniture. She was completely oblivious to what was taking place. I picked her up and handed her to my mother. She touched her face as if to say goodbye.

As we drove away from my childhood home, I cried my tears of frustration. All these years of struggling to rebuild my relationship with my mom only to have the visit end like this. A fight over fucking food. Why? I was shaking my head. How could the visit end any other way? Things had come full circle in my family. I was no longer the person who needed to be helped. I was no longer a young woman in need of a rescue. I wasn't begging to come back home. I was a strong, independent woman with a loving family of my own. It wasn't the meal that made her upset. It was the fact that no one was left who she felt needed her.

When the plane touched down, I called my mother immediately. I felt so horrible that we'd had a stupid fight.

"Mom," I told her, "I am hoping you are okay. I am home and I love you."

I could hear that she had been crying.

"I am proud of you, Tracey," she told me in a soft voice. "I ate the food. It was delicious. How did you make it?"

Just like that, we were back in our familiar territory. There were no resentments, just forgiveness. Life was too short to stay angry.

My relationship with her would never be without conflict. We were both stubborn people. As a child, I had always dreamed about the things I wanted to change about her. One of the gifts of recovery is that I could accept her. The person I needed to change was myself. If I spent my time focusing on all the things I could not have, I would never feel satisfied with my life.

Some people feel that addicts don't have the ability to care about anyone but themselves. Addiction is not a state of apathy. Addiction is the place where the user loses the inability to find a solution to the broader problem. Yes, I was aware that my arm was falling off from an abscess. Yes, I was aware that I had not seen my family for years. Yes, I was aware that I was completely isolated by continued use of a substance. But solving those problems seemed completely beyond my daily abilities. In recovery, I focus on my smaller realities. When I think about the next day, the next week, the next month, I feel overwhelmed by my responsibilities. When I break my life into smaller events, however, I can see and measure my progress. By focusing on little achievements, I incrementally build an entirely new existence for myself.

I never could have realized that trip would be the last time I would see my parents. My father slipped in and out of illnesses until he finally passed away while I was in the hospital giving birth to my second child in April of 2009. It was an eerie feeling to have these events happen at nearly the exact same moment. I was numb, literally, from the pain medication, and figuratively from the feeling of knowing he was gone.

Four months later, I received a call from my sister. It was about my mother. She was hospitalized, diagnosed, and died that week. Living so far away, I was lucky my brother and sister could be there for her. After forty-seven years of ups and downs, I should have guessed my mother would be ready to join my father. I was told by a neighbor that when he died, she had said she "lost her purpose." My siblings and I found out that my mother had been walking around for months or possibly years with leukemia. By the time she entered the hospital, she had advanced to stage four.

My last interaction with my mother was a hurried phone call in between lab tests. She had been in and out of consciousness for a few days. The doctors had predicted she might last another month. I was making a plan to get there before she passed on. I had my flight booked. Yet in my heart I felt like I would never make it. I knew her. I knew she was ready to let go.

"Mom," I told her, "I am coming to see you next week."

"Tracey . . ." she said weakly. "See if you can get a refund on my tickets. I hate to have you spend the money." She was just a few weeks out from a trip she had just booked to San Francisco with my sister, to meet her new grandson. She would never make it.

"I got my tickets to Ohio already, Mom. I just want you to understand," I explained. "I want to make sure you understand how much I love you."

I could hear the nurses enter the room as she told me, "I love you too, sweetheart." We had a few minutes more to talk before she had to go get more tests.

I was sitting in my office at work. I hung up the phone. She died two days later. My mother was gone. She slipped away before I'd gotten the chance to see her. Fortunately, I had spent the last eleven years telling her how I felt. But hearing her, knowing that cancer was eating her alive, I felt peace in letting her go. The process certainly wasn't easy. It was painful and scary and lonely. But she had prepared me for this moment. She had loved me. She had guided me to a place where I was a woman who was strong enough to stand on my own, even if it was painful for her at times to let me go.

I caught her in one of the last moments when she was present. I would like to believe she had hung on long enough to tell me goodbye. When I saw her in the casket, I knew she was no longer there. I had avoided other memorials for lovers, for friends, coworkers, and clients. But I dealt with her passing head on. I touched her hand. Her makeup was atrocious—no one could ever match that overdone foundation and blush my mother had painted on her whole life. I reached into the casket to touch her hand. I gave her back the wedding ring she had first put on her hand forty-seven years earlier. I slipped it carefully on her finger. It was the last thing I could do for her.

In a sense, I had been telling her "hello" and "goodbye" for the past eleven years. For eleven years, she was my best friend. I had been a junkie, a prostitute, a thief, and a liar. These things were true. I could not change any of them. All I could do was live in the present. I was also her daughter. As I had learned to forgive myself, I had learned how to accept love. As painful as the death of my mother was, I never considered using drugs. The sadness was something I was able to accept. Not because I didn't care, but because I knew, in my heart, I had made the most out of those eleven years together.

In the years since I had quit drugs, there had been a vacation to Hawaii, a trip to Vegas, my graduation from college, and many nights spent chatting on the phone. There were no words that were unsaid between my mother and myself. There were no awkward pauses. She made me into the woman I had become. I was a strong person. I picked up my children and squeezed them tightly as we walked out of the church. There was no fucking way I was going to use, today or any other day. My children gave me a reason to continue. Just like my mother, my children gave me a reason to live. I kissed both of their faces as I loaded them into their car seats.

Chapter 11

A GOOD DAY

My day ends like any other day. Lots of screaming, lots of chaos.

I feel whiskers on my cheek. "Hi," my husband, home from work, says as he kisses me.

If he is home, it must be 5:20 PM. I am going to need his help. I need to get three kids fed, bathed, and in bed by 8:00 PM. The countdown starts. Most of the time, I fail at this target, but I am not aiming at perfection. I am aiming at survival. All those years as a street-level drug addict have prepared me for the challenge of a busy life as a mother.

It feels like I haven't gotten a good night's sleep in three years. But all those years on methamphetamine had prepared me for the first child who refused to sleep through the night. All those years of homelessness have allowed me to take a nap anywhere, at any time. I am not above putting my head on my desk, lying down on the floor, or catching a few fleeting moments on the train. I started out as a mom who swore up and down I would never let my children watch TV. I had more than one argument with my mother about it. When I look back, I laugh at myself. Now, I call it the TV sitter. I use it to help me catch my breath in a busy moment. These little lives are depending on me to get this routine right without losing my mind. It seems hard to believe how we got to this place. Children were just a dream to me. Now, I have three little smiling faces that all call me Mommy.

I pour myself a half cup of coffee as I make my rounds. Yes, it is nighttime, but I still need "mother's little helper." I let the dog out into our backyard. It still seems strange to say it: *our* backyard. Where we live isn't a room. It isn't an apartment. Christian and I pooled our limited resources together to buy a home outside the city. I used to sit in the twelve-step meetings and hear the speaker say, "I went from homeless to homeowner," never imagining that could be me. I had many goals in recovery. Living in the Bay Area, I had never felt this one was attainable. Many times Christian and I had discussed the idea. Many times I squashed it with my negativity. When we were handed the keys, a few months before the birth of my second son, I was in awe of how much my life had truly changed. At first, for financial reasons, we had to take on a housemate. But within a few months we were able to catch up and live on our own. I now live two miles from the ocean. On summer nights when the fog rolls in, I remember that feeling of being homeless in 1992. I would huddle next to some other homeless kid for warmth as we tried to dodge the sea breeze.

Meetings are not a big part of my life anymore. It's not that I ever think to myself, *Oh, I am over those meetings.* I still go periodically. Perhaps five or six times a year I read materials related to my recovery. I stay in touch with old friends from the program. I don't think I am cured of my addiction. I got clean to have a life. Now I'm living that life—a life full of purpose. I share my recovery with the hope of being of service to others struggling with addiction. Over the years, some friends have been able to successfully transition to appropriate drinking. Some have chosen to stay abstinent. There are those who have relapsed, only to return. More than a few have died with a needle next to them, or in them. That is the pitfall of loving an addict. You have no control over their choices.

"Katie," I gently shake my daughter. "Katie-bear. It's time to brush your teeth."

I hear some mumbling and know that she heard me. She is the easiest to get moving on the bedtime routine. She loves school. That alone will get her to bed: She wants to wake up in the morning and go see her friends. When I see her face, I wonder what I was like at this age. Every addict was once an innocent child, a son or a daughter. We didn't wake up one day, then decide to stick a needle in our neck. There was this whole series of events that ended in the epic struggle over dependence on a substance. What can I say to her that might make a difference? Is there some magical phrase that will keep her drug free? It pains me to think that there might be some gene I have passed on to her that, once activated, could lead her down the same path.

Time to move to the next station. As I go to get the boys motivated, the cat almost knocks me over. When I look at my boys, I wonder what it is I can say to make them into caring young men. I fear for them, too, that they will pick up my addictive habits. More importantly, I wonder how I can keep them from becoming like the violent men I had in my past. How can I nurture them in a way that will bring out their compassion instead of the need to control? Being a parent has completely shifted the world around me. I never thought I had the ability to change or impact anything. Through the eyes of my children, I see the tremendous difference I can make by being present in their lives.

A few hours later, I turn on the light in the boys' room. For a moment, I catch a glimpse of their sleeping faces. My youngest son just recently started sleeping in his crib every night. It seemed as if it was always easier to keep him in our room. I don't know if he actually slept better, but I know I slept better not being woken up by my husband returning to our bed after settling the new baby. Those years of sleeping in alleyways have made me an extremely light sleeper. Unfortunately, the sound of my husband's snoring is enough to wake the neighbors. I had taken to sleeping with earplugs over the course of our relationship. Now, I need to be able to hear the children crying. I am forced to poke him as my only recourse. I suppose sometimes it feels good to shake the bed and wake him up. As a person who loved heroin, I hate that feeling of not being able to sleep. Heroin for me was one long dream state interrupted by painful reality. My life today is the reality I always dreamed of.

I used to hear the line, "You can't turn a hoe into a housewife." I certainly have proven that isn't true. I have broken all the stereotypes about what a woman can achieve. I am a mother, a boss, a homeowner. In fact, I am one badass bitch, to use another phrase from my past. It is amazing to me how I have adapted to functioning in this new life. It is almost as if all those years of living out on the street prepared me for my most important role: being a mother. I try to see my past as one big education. I can't change the things I have done. I can't undo my mistakes. I can only evolve from them. I have evolved into a caring human being who savors every moment. I am blessed by the new life I created for myself.

I swoop up the Netflix envelope and pop in a DVD. My husband and I have one quiet hour together before we have to start all over again.

In the morning, we get back into our zone. Nursing a baby, eating breakfast, and drinking a few sips of coffee. I am a master at multitasking. Sometimes I am so tired in the morning, I have to catch myself from putting my coffee cup on the baby's head while he is nursing. While I am zoned out, it seems like a logical resting spot. I need these five minutes to watch the weather report. Any type of rain requires extra time, time I do not have in the morning. Sometimes my husband can go into work a little later in the morning and help change and dress at least two out of three. Other days, he does the routine. Alas, today is not one of those days. At least there is no rain in the forecast. I take comfort in the little blessings.

And that moment is over as my son calls, "Mommy, I'm wet!"

His diaper leaked a little in the night. He insists on drinking water before bedtime, which creates havoc in the morning. I kiss my baby son and set him down with a toy. He isn't really a baby anymore, I suppose, at a little over one year old. But he is still my baby—my last child. I had my tubes tied to shut down my baby insanity. I am just shy of forty-two years old with three little kids. I change my middle son and strip the sheets off the race-car bed. Add another five minutes to my routine. The time is slipping away from me. Not unlike those moments when I needed my drugs and I had to make something happen for myself. I know how to react under pressure. I know how to manage my time wisely. I know how to be patient. I can manage this and much more with the love of my family.

"I don't want that shirt," my son insists. He tries to push my hand away.

The struggle to be independent starts so soon.

"I want Batman, not Elmo," he says.

You will give in long before they will. My mother's words echo in my ears.

My mistake—I seem to always be a day behind the new likes and dislikes of my children. Unfortunately, I cannot always accommodate their radical changes in taste. I am willing to try this morning, to no avail. Of course, Batman is in the laundry. Many of their favorite things seem to always be in the laundry. The struggle to get my daughter dressed seems to be an endless exercise in pushing the rock up the hill. On a chilly, foggy Daly City morning, sandals and sundresses will be ruled out as appropriate wardrobe choices. This will result in crying, pouting, or perhaps screaming at me. At least she can dress herself. We settle on an outfit of the mismatched variety. Stripes and polka dots seem fine to her as long as they're both pink. We arrive at a more muted selection of sparkly Hello Kitty top and jeans. The battle over jeans seems to be score one for Team Mom. I am not sure who she is competing with in terms of the battle to be most fashionable, but she clearly feels this is a battle she must win. I might wear the same outfit four days in a row if I don't have to face the public. Three C-sections have left me with limited options, with an exploding muffin top where I once had a waist.

I feel a sense of accomplishment. Two out of three children are dressed! Oh wait, I still haven't changed the baby. I sit on the couch and put him on a changing pad on the floor; I do this whenever possible to save the stress on my back from lifting him. Fortunately, I laid out his clothes last night. Well, this is sort of true—I had actually dozed off while folding clothes. I did not get a chance to put them away. If my middle son was more educated in the domestic arts, he would tear the laundry basket apart looking for his Batman shirt, which must be buried somewhere at the bottom. For now, he sees the laundry as a magical location where clothes disappear, return folded, and are then placed in his drawer. I try to manipulate him into changing his mind about his shirt while I dress the youngest.

We still haven't gotten to breakfast. Lately I have fallen into the habit of searching for the most convenient of breakfast items. The main staples seem to be anything that is mashed and placed in a pouch. Crushers, or whatever they are called, seem to be a busy mom's best friend. They are like baby crack. My kids can eat four of them in three minutes, and there goes $5 up in smoke. Sounds like crack to me. I should know. I really have to thank crack, though. If it wasn't for crack, maybe I wouldn't be here today. Heroin kept me chasing my tail, but crack finally sent me into recovery. Thanks, crack!

My thoughts are interrupted. "Mommy, I'm hungry." I have snuck off to use the bathroom, by myself (shocking), and now I have a little hand pounding at the door. Clearly, the food isn't stored in here. I'm attempting to use the toilet while checking my emails. Even though it's before 6:00 AM, people from work are already texting me. Someone is calling in sick, so I need to arrange coverage. All the elements in my life are overlapping in a symphony of stress. I whisper to myself, "I've got this." I have been through worse things. Managing the morning is nothing compared to almost having my leg fall off from an infection. That memory helps put things into perspective.

In the kitchen, I pour out a bowl of Cheerios for the kids to share. I set them on the floor in front of the TV while I surf for a show that will grab their attention. I need these twenty-two minutes to get myself together. I need to put in my contacts, get dressed, and get on their kids' shoes and jackets while they are still transfixed by *Wallykazam!* or *Team Umizoomi*. I exhale when I see the clock. There is just not enough time in the day.

As I sort through my pile of clothes, I get confused by the garments. What have I already worn this week? The clothes are no longer on hangers. I will sort them back into some kind of order on the weekend. My life is so similar to the life of other moms, yet many of my choices have been so different. In selecting an outfit, I need to make sure I cover up my track marks and my scars. The abscess scars that pepper my arms and legs cannot be obvious today. I have a presentation to do and I want to make a good impression. Maybe no one sees them, but I know they are there. I see my scars as important reminders of how far I have come in life. I have lived so close to death, yet I am here to tell the tale. Like the junkie phoenix, I rise from the ashes. I take my place in the sun.

Sometimes it is hard to believe that was ever my life. I started out drinking socially as a teenager and ended up a homeless junkie in the streets of San Francisco. My journey between these two places was not unlike my morning with the kids. I woke up from a fog and thought, *How did I get here?* The clear difference is that in recovery I do the exact opposite of things I did while I was on drugs. I am able to examine my attitudes and my behaviors and come up with solutions. Rather than being ruled by my insecurities, I can face the future with compassion for myself.

When I go to put my clothes on for work, I frequently take a moment to breathe a sigh of relief. In that moment, I know my day is full of opportunities. The gratitude I feel puts things into focus. This house, these kids, this life: It is all mine. What a gift. I plan to put it to use. My day is full of the promise. I had so many days in my past when I struggled just to survive. On these quiet mornings in my little home where my only audience is three adoring children, I take a moment to pray for the strength to make a difference today. I have created my own affirmation that helps me put my life in perspective:

> *I woke up this morning. I was in a bed. This is a good start to any morning.*
>
> *I had food to eat. Another goal accomplished.*
>
> *I was able to use the bathroom indoors. Yes.*
>
> *I texted with a friend and got out some resentments.*
>
> *I felt my feelings.*
>
> *Most of all, I am not digging into my neck, hands, or feet for a place to inject my daily emotions.*
>
> *I am clean—a good start to the day.*

I hear some commotion in the next room. Children can be little savages prone to violence. One second they are watching TV, the next second they are smacking each other over the last of the cereal.

"Mommy!" I hear my call to arms. "Eddie is eating all the Cheerios!"

As quickly as the moment of reflection came into my mind, the moment passes. I need to focus on completing the tasks of the morning. Hopefully, I can make it through the last part of our morning ritual without getting food stains from little fingers on my dress pants. There is also the matter of hair brushing that must be tackled. This is an area I prefer to defer to my husband whenever humanly possible. The screaming involved per stroke of the brush increases my level of annoyance exponentially as I am simply trying to help my daughter. In her mind, this whole process is some form of torture uniquely designed by me to ruin her day.

If only I had more time today to spend with each of them individually. If only I had more time to tell them how much I love them. I have come to the conclusion that I did receive love from my parents, but somewhere along the line I never learned how to love myself. When I discovered that the solution was inside me, I no longer felt broken. I felt teachable. I felt hopeful. It was a process to restore myself to a condition of wholeness. Perhaps I never felt whole. But I now know that I will never allow a substance or a man or a poor choice to dictate my image of myself again. I feel good about myself because I work hard at doing positive things. I want the same for my children.

The yelling starts. "STOP it!" I hear from the next room.

There is a battle over shutting off the TV. My son likes to play with the buttons. If we can make it out the door in the morning, I feel as if I have won some personal battle. As all three kids assemble at the door, I take one final look at the house. Our home is filled with the evidence of happy children and busy parents. I have packed the breakfast snacks, I have packed my lunch, and everyone is dressed and ready for their day.

Outside, as I lock the door, my son asks, "Mommy, will you hold my hand?"

Of course I will, son. We are in this together.

I start dropping off my kids in anxious anticipation of the day ahead. I have a new hire to meet with, my presentation, and one-to-one sessions lined up with each of the staff. The program I run has grown so quickly. I now supervise seventeen staff people, each of whom I'm training to be a peer counselor. Our lived experience bridges the gap within county services. It is a blessing to be able to take all my negative experiences and use them to help someone.

Slowly but surely, I have gotten back into harm reduction as a way to be of service. The death of my mother left a hole in my life. There will be no more Sunday phone calls. I can no longer ask her for advice. I miss her sense of humor. I disagreed with her on politics, social issues, and television shows. When she died, I found pictures she had taken from a Sarah Palin rally. I laughed my ass off. I wish I could have had the chance to ask her why someone who voted for Kennedy and Carter was at a Sarah Palin rally. We ran out of time. The space that was left by her death can't be filled with drugs, food, or self-pity. I filled that hole with action. I knew I wanted to be of service to the community at large. I started receiving messages from users, their friends, and their families seeking information on heroin. Over the course of a few months, I found myself in a role where I feel comfortable— sharing my story of recovery for the benefit of others.

After I drop off my daughter, I quickly push the stroller and rush to the train. We have caught the magic bullet that will get me to work just in time. On the train, as we get close to our stop, my son points to a homeless man. It has been drizzling outside, typical for a Bay Area morning despite the forecast. The man sits near the door and has a shopping cart with all his belongings next to him. Soon the police will make him move. I remember those mornings when I rode the train for a safe place to sleep.

"Mommy," my son asks, "why is that man eating on the train?"

I look over to see the man eating a few crackers. It is clear he wants to blend into the shadows. His safety comes from being ignored. Humanity comes from being acknowledged.

"He is homeless and probably hungry," I tell him.

"What does that mean?" he asks urgently.

I sigh. This is not an easy conversation.

"Eddie," I explain, "he doesn't have a place to live. Mommy was once homeless like him. Long before you were born."

This is as far as we get in these conversations. My children are too young to understand what "homeless" means, and what it means to use "drugs." I get asked in emails, "What will you tell your children about your drug use?" I will attempt to be as honest with them as possible. I think it is essential to tell my truth. Rather than hide things from them, I hope my story will help educate them. When we are at social events, my children sometimes ask about beer. Why do adults drink beer if kids can't drink it? Mommy doesn't drink beer. To me, that is the lesson: It doesn't matter what other people do; I make healthy choices for myself by choosing not to have one.

As we stand up to get off the train, my son hands me his breakfast bar.

"Mommy, I don't want this."

I see the man with the shopping cart smiling at my children. I grab the snack and hand it to him. His face lights up.

"Thank you," he tells me in a hushed voice as he rips open the snack.

My kids look confused as we step off the train.

"My cook-cooks," Kelan mumbles. He is referring to his breakfast "cookies."

"He needed them more," I tell the boys. I pat their heads and point them toward the elevator.

I hand off my sons to the babysitter with a tight hug and a kiss. Leaving them is painful. I looked into being a stay-at home mom, but the numbers were not in my favor. Between a mortgage payment and health care costs, my husband and I must both work full time. I try to take a day off every few weeks to spend with the kids. They won't be this age much longer. Katie has just started kindergarten. The time has gone by so quickly. It wasn't so long ago she was a tiny baby swinging in my arms. Recently I joined the PTA at the school. My journey from drug-addicted criminal to active community member has been a long one. Between the gymnastics, the dance classes, and soccer, the only bags I deal with anymore contain uniforms and special shoes. I am a changed person.

In the end, I found that, for me, there was no big fix. There was no food, no drug, no relationship, no program alone that could fix the things I didn't like about myself. My life was transformed incrementally when I dedicated myself to pursuing something beyond instant gratification. With seventeen years clean, I still have periodic patches of depression. I was diagnosed with anxiety in 2012. There are times when it is as much a struggle to get out the door as it was in those days in my room in the Tenderloin.

I may have more material things, but probably less than the average person would suspect. When I go on a business trip, I rarely need more than a backpack.

I plan to visit with my siblings this year. I know this would make my mother happy. We have never been a close bunch, but in the end, we are still a family. I have also grown to love my in-laws. I never thought I could love anything besides heroin. Fortunately, I was very, very wrong.

This is my life today. As I walk through the farmers' market on the way to work, I see the "home bums"—lifetime alcoholics, not necessarily homeless, who prefer to drink outside—sipping their morning medicine. I recognize a few faces. Sometimes they say hello to me. Sometimes they hide their faces in glassy-eyed embarrassment. To see the way many of my companions have aged is enough to bring a tear to my eye. I see the mother who has lost all four of her children to the system. I see the man who walked away from his family after a relapse. I walk behind the man I once had a youthful crush on, now devoid of any teeth or dignity. The crowd has gotten much older here. It seems as if the world of drugs has gotten much harder for these people on the streets. There are fewer places to be an unbridled addict. The hustlers on Polk Street have been replaced by hipsters. The dark net markets make it possible to sell your body and buy your drugs in relative privacy. That's what the young hookers tell me. The world I knew has dissolved into pieces. I am still part of it, yet I am completely removed from the struggle. I step over someone who is passed out in front of Starbucks. I have to get to work. I know I will see you when I pass by here again.

PART
TWO

BEYOND THE WAR
ON DRUGS

Getting off drugs wasn't an individual effort. Sure, I could easily take the credit. "Hey, look at me. I was living next to a Dumpster on a pissy blanket when suddenly I decided to put the drugs behind me! I wanted a different life. From the day I went to jail, I never relapsed. I did it!" That would make for a convenient story—that pick-yourself-up-by-your-bootstraps narrative that the media loves—but that was not my experience. I was responsible for making the decision to stop using drugs. I can own that accomplishment. However, it's important to acknowledge the significant roles other people and organizations played in my recovery, and to understand the vast amount of work that must still be done so more can experience recovery. To me, it made all the difference that there were people who treated me like I was still a human being during times when I was living like an animal.

For me, recovery wasn't an overnight process—it was a series of events dating back to my active using days—but my journey started at the needle exchange. The very first person I met who had successfully kicked heroin and stayed off for many years was a staff person at the exchange. By talking with us, encouraging us, and simply being there, the staff and volunteers reinforced that all drug users are human beings, deserving of compassion. They provided me with clean supplies for injection, as well as condoms. That made it possible for me to make it through the 1990s without contracting the HIV virus or an STD. I had been an IV drug user for a while before I started using the needle exchange; I was sharing used needles with friends and lovers, with little concern for my health and safety. Needle exchange did not encourage me to use, as some have argued. It allowed me to use safely. The main difference between my friends who died and those who remained free of the virus was the consistent use of safe injection supplies and condoms. Before meeting the staff at the exchange, I can't recall ever having had safe sex. After attending a workshop there, it became my general practice.

Syringe exchange can also prevent a myriad of medical conditions, including HIV, hepatitis C, endocarditis, and soft tissue infections. But in the U.S., in terms of syringe sales and exchange programs, our public health policies have actually gone backward: Funding for such programs is banned at the federal level. In many states, it is a crime just to possess a syringe without a prescription, and even in states where it isn't, many users still report that pharmacies refuse to sell them syringes. HIV infection rates are actually going up in Miami and certain communities in Indiana. After a recent cluster of HIV cases broke out in Indiana, it took a state emergency order to get a needle exchange program in place. In addition, there are frequently no proper avenues for disposal of the syringes, which are hazardous medical waste. I am a living example of why we need to lift the federal ban on syringe exchange.

I also give a lot of credit to public health clinics like the ones I went to in San Francisco, which provide health care for the homeless and made it possible for me to progress in my recovery. No clinic ever asked me to leave because of my disheveled appearance. No one ever turned me away for being a junkie. Conversely, when I was sleeping outside, local residents would sometimes pour bleach on me from their apartment windows while screaming slurs at me. I had people throw bottles at me, laugh at me, throw trash at me. I was made to feel less than human. But the public health workers I encountered reassured me through their actions that someone cared for my well-being. I remember a long conversation I once had with a doctor at a health center who commended my efforts at trying to take care of one of my wounds despite my living on the streets. Twenty years later, this doctor is now one of my coworkers. When I think of how I want to treat others, I frequently reflect back on my experiences at that health center.

The clinic was also a place where I could openly discuss my issues with drugs and alcohol. I didn't have to hide any of my medical history. Because I was able to speak my truth, I was supported in making positive health choices. The clinic staff provided me with alternatives to the grind of daily use. They discussed ways to reduce my intake while giving me information on available services in the community.

Many users who contact me fear (or have had) the opposite experience. They are terrified to disclose to medical professionals any portion of their addiction history. They're afraid of repercussions at their place of employment, from their parents under whose health plans they're covered, and from the health care professionals themselves. Expanding substance abuse services provided in the primary care setting could go a long way toward destigmatization and reducing the harm caused by both legal drugs and illicit substances. Managed health care organizations could provide peer educators on-site who offer confidential counseling, education, and referrals that are not linked to a person's general medical record.

The next critical step in my journey was medication-assisted treatment (MAT). MAT offered me an alternative to my routine of injecting heroin six to eight times a day. Methadone is one such treatment—it's the most heavily researched and widely used. It is often called the "gold standard" for MAT. But my experience with the long lines at the methadone clinic reminded me of my time in jail, when inmates were herded like cattle anytime they needed food, medication, or to move around.

The first time I went to the methadone clinic, my only goal was to stop using heroin on a daily basis. Methadone allowed me to detox from heroin at my own pace instead of going cold turkey. I paid $12 a day to get my medication. I had to "dose" every single day at the clinic for twenty-one straight days. The dosage was reduced daily until I completed the detox. As a direct result of the methadone, I was able to quit heroin for three months. I was able to stop supporting my habit with sex work. I was able to let my scars heal, to make a few friends. While some would argue I wasn't really "clean," that wasn't actually my goal at first. It was an important stepping-stone and an early success because I was able to temporarily quit using drugs on a daily basis as a direct result of the program.

When I returned to methadone treatment after a five-year absence, I had to find a different clinic. My new one was surrounded by people selling pills, heroin, and crack. The police were constantly surveilling the area around the clinic. As a private pay client, I received no counseling. Clients who were on public benefits were forced to sit through weekly counseling, even if they had been clean for years. I was told this was so the clinic could bill the government the maximum amount for that patient. I was required to pay daily and be at the clinic by 2:00 PM every day or I would not receive my medication. At the time, I was paying $35 per day to live in a hotel, and my rent was due by noon. By the time I gathered enough money to pay for my room or else face being homeless, there was not always enough money to pay for my methadone. After a few days of missing my dose, I quit going to the clinic. I wanted to stop using, but I could not afford it or manage to keep going to the clinic. I faced brutal withdrawals from this long-lasting opiate therapy.

From my observations, the methadone clinic system is antiquated and cumbersome. It is widely known as "liquid handcuffs." Methadone requires daily dosing, per federal requirements, every single day for ninety days, unless a patient is lucky enough to live in a state where the clinic is closed on the weekends. It may take a patient a few years to be able to accumulate the benefits and switch to once-a-week dosing. While working in a hospital-based clinic for over four years, I was shocked at the level of bureaucracy involved in getting a client even one take-home dose of methadone. I once overheard a client tell another person in the elevator, "I have had to come here almost every day for the past eight years." I was disgusted by this. Whether or not the patient is "clean," the system creates an unfair burden on him or her. There is little incentive for addicts to completely discontinue use of illicit drugs when we tell them at the outset, "We don't trust you enough to manage your own medications."

Buprenorphine, another opiate replacement therapy, is also a powerful medication that allows patients to make sensible choices about their medical care without excessive rules and regulations. It was in the trial stage at a clinic in San Francisco during a time when I was considering my options for treatment, and I had some friends who participated in the trial. I was impressed by how much freedom people in the trial seemed to enjoy with buprenorphine compared to daily dosing of methadone. They were treated as if they had a medical issue (which it was), not a criminal one. The patients had the freedom to go for days without visiting a clinic. Because addiction is now treated as a chronic medical condition, patients today can use buprenorphine and other newer medical interventions with fewer restrictions. With buprenorphine, in a relatively short period of time, the patient may be able to receive a month's worth of take-home medication.

Not to say there are no issues with buprenorphine. I hear reports of doctors refusing to prescribe the much cheaper generic form of the medication. With HMOs, there may be only a handful of plan doctors, leaving hundreds of patients on the waiting list. In private practice, the costs for the medication can be quite prohibitive, including $450 for the initial visit, plus hundreds more for office visits, urine tests, and blood work. Many providers refuse insurance because their waiting rooms are full of patients willing to pay cash. For patients desperate to get off opiates, the monthly cost of MAT can easily surpass that of food, rent, or a car payment.

My hope is that we can reform these systems to make them more affordable, more equitable, and more patient friendly. Despite the potentially high profit margins for providers, waiting lists can take months. In some states, like Kentucky, concerns around buphrenorphine "pill mills" have even caused some clinics to close or severely restrict the number of patients an individual practice can take. There is no shortage of need, only a shortage of hope.

In the final piece of my journey to recovery, I was ready to commit to total abstinence from all drugs. I perceived this to be my last chance. I felt as if I had tried everything else. I'd been offered the chance to go to treatment a few years prior, but I refused—I didn't want my parents to have to take out a second mortgage on their home to send me to rehab. At that time, I knew I was not going to stop using drugs. This was my reality. When I was finally ready, I was lucky. I was able to stay in a residential treatment facility for a little over ninety days. This gave me enough time to learn to cope with my emotions. This gave me enough time to learn how to avoid people who were using. This gave me enough time to find both a job and stable housing. Even if I wasn't completely "ready" to leave at the end, I had a good start.

In today's environment, ninety days in rehab is a junkie unicorn—a fantasy for anyone without money. The standard stay in treatment is only twenty-eight to thirty days. As private insurance companies and government-run programs like Medicaid look to cut costs, it appears there is an emphasis on quantity of patients over quality of care. While more patients are churned through the system, there is little work being done to verify patient outcomes. Generally, this information is provided through self-report, which can be extremely unreliable considering the sensitive nature of substance abuse. In addition, short-term inpatient rehab is barely enough time for an opiate user to be able to recover from post-acute withdrawal syndrome, or PAWS. PAWS happens in the period after detoxification during which users may experience anxiety, mood swings, low energy, depression, and, in the worst-case scenario, thoughts of suicide. They may discover they have some condition that they've been covering up with drugs, and feel the impulse to self-injure. If I had gone through shorter-term rehab, by the time I started to feel a little better, it would have been time to go! Aftercare, if offered, is often both minimal and optional. Even after ninety days in rehab, I completed another three months of aftercare and just short of four years in a sober living environment (SLE).

SLEs, which generally are not covered by insurance, are houses managed by a former resident or another person in recovery. The rules vary as much as the amenities do. The SLE I lived in was made up of single rooms in an old converted hotel in one of the worst areas of San Francisco. I received no counseling, but was required to attend church or twelve-step meetings during my first year. My rent was kept low with the hopes that I would save money to transition into my own place. There was no kitchen, a shared bathroom down the hall, and broken furniture. It was perfect for me at the time, though I had numerous friends balk at the mere suggestion of moving there.

There is little in the way of regulation and standardization in the SLE industry. The barriers to starting an SLE are nearly nonexistent, and the need is great. What constitutes a sober living house? Even with the research I did, it was difficult to find an answer to that. Anyone with a rental property can open a building and call it sober living. This is confusing and dangerous for those seeking substantial support after treatment. Some have rigid standards by which a resident can be put out in the street on the same day he or she has a positive urine test. Some have no real system for locking up medications, making theft commonplace. There are sober living places that look like luxury apartments, while others have parolees stacked in bunk beds. If the period after treatment can be the most dangerous time, then we need some standardization in programming to safely house those who are trying to stay clean.

My sober living program was based on the idea that the twelve-step program was the only way to stay clean. I will freely admit, there were days when twelve-step meetings were my sole reason for leaving my room. However, I question the need to *require* twelve-step meetings as a condition for residency in any program. I may seem critical of the twelve-step program, but this criticism is not without merit. Although it was an important framework for my recovery, it wasn't the sole reason for it. And there were times in twelve-step when I found myself in situations that could have had some serious consequences. On several occasions, I received inaccurate information and even worse advice. I was the victim of predatory behavior of males in the meetings. I was exposed to an ideology of forgiveness of others that directly clashed with my efforts to cope with PTSD.

When alternatives to twelve-step are available, I feel strongly that those seeking recovery should have the right to pursue what works for them. I cringe at the "one-size-fits-all" approach, because I have seen what happens when it fails too many times.

I received this email from a parent after many months of correspondence. She was looking for a way to help her son who had tried to be other people's idea of "clean":

> *Hi Tracey: My son didn't survive. I feel like he might have tapered off too soon. It wasn't long before I found him. He was dead. He had been out drinking with his friends. He just wanted to be like everyone else. I can't blame him. I thought he was doing well. He went back to*

school, he sounded fine. No one knew he had relapsed. My son died all alone as a result of this disease.

Whether or not we agree that addiction is a "disease" as discussed in twelve-step literature, we can agree that the premature death of a person is a tragedy. Think of all the lives that were touched by this young man. His family, his friends, his teachers, his neighbors are all left with that feeling: *What could I have done to save him?* The answer could have come in the form of naloxone, if only he'd had access to it. Naloxone, commonly known under the name Narcan, is used to temporarily reverse the effects of an opiate overdose, often saving the person's life. While it may not be effective in every instance, it is an inexpensive tool slowly becoming available to the general public.

As deaths from opiate overdose reach epidemic proportions, including naloxone in standard first aid kits could save thousands of lives. Most people who have overdosed were with someone else who potentially could have saved them. Naloxone kits were not available when I was using heroin, but I certainly would have carried one. Even though I have never experienced a relapse since leaving treatment, I certainly have experienced the pain of losing people close to me. In late 1998, I was casually reading a newspaper when I came across an article about the rash of fatal overdoses in San Francisco. Among those names, I saw my friend, Jennifer. She was a beautiful person, a bright soul. She had written me a letter of encouragement when I was in jail. I lost many friends before Jennifer, and after. But her death inspired me to action. Since 1999, I have worked to prevent overdose deaths. Although Jennifer was found alone, there was a high probability someone was with her when she began to overdose. This was a person who might have saved Jennifer's life if he or she had been willing and equipped to get involved.

We've made progress in the U.S., but there are still many states with *no* naloxone programs and *no* Good Samaritan laws that offer specific protections related to overdose. In the years I was using, I performed CPR on five different people to revive them from overdoses. In one case in particular, I performed CPR with rescue breathing to the point of exhaustion. I was about to give up on her when, fortunately, the paramedics arrived—with a police escort. I was threatened with being taken to jail because I was using heroin. I was appropriately responding to a medical emergency! My first thought when I found this woman should not have been "Should I leave her?" because I was afraid of going to jail for my involvement.

Calling 911 with no legal repercussions, increasing distribution of naloxone, and supporting education about overdose are key pieces in the chain of survival. In my work distributing naloxone, I've seen how easy it can be to save a life when people have the proper tools. I've also seen how difficult it can be when nothing is there to help users in their time of need.

Addicts cannot get clean if they are dead. How many more lives will be needlessly lost before we create more commonsense health policies in the United States? While for many my story has been one of hope, I think of it as a call for action. In the time it has taken for you to read this book, how many people died because they had no access to naloxone? What infections were caused because people had no access to clean needles? How many family members were unable to sleep as they waited up to learn whether their loved one was safe after being kicked out of rehab? I don't see myself as an extraordinary person. I see myself as an ordinary person highlighting things many are afraid to share. We can all do something to make a difference. We can get involved by telling our stories, by demanding change.

Someday, when I am gone, I hope my children will be proud of me. I hope they won't remember me as their mom, the heroin addict. I want them to think of me as a person who loved them unconditionally, who worked to benefit my community, who saved lives. How will you be remembered? Instead of holding in our fears for our loved ones, instead of holding in our grief, we have a unique opportunity to create change. I hope you will join me by bringing your voice, your experiences, and your truth to the conversations and movements for a better world.

PART
THREE

HEROIN ADDICTION & RECOVERY: WHAT YOU NEED TO KNOW

WHAT IS HEROIN?

To understand a heroin user, you must first begin to understand something about the drug that is controlling his or her life. Heroin is one in a variety of opioids, all of which are abusable with a little bit of determination. The general public is more familiar with prescription opiates such as Oxy-Contin, Vicodin, Norco, morphine, Dilaudid, Percocet, and fentanyl. If you have had a medical procedure in the U.S., the chances are high that you have been prescribed one of these medications.

Heroin is not so different from these prescription drugs. According to the National Institute on Drug Abuse (www.drug abuse.gov/publications/research-reports/heroin/letter-director), "Heroin is an illegal, highly addictive drug processed from morphine, a naturally occurring substance extracted from the seed pod of certain varieties of poppy plants. Once heroin enters the brain, it is converted to morphine and binds rapidly to opioid receptors." Heroin fills the pleasure center of your brain, creating a feeling of euphoria. Depending on the way it is ingested, known as the route of administration, the onset of this feeling can be extremely intense, often referred to as a "rush." In the worst-case scenario, the rush can overpower the systems of the body, slowing functioning to the point of an overdose. The breathing and heart rate slow down as death sets in from lack of oxygen. In the best-case scenario, a high from heroin can last most of the day. The user falls into a sleeplike state known as a "nod," or in some cases, the user reports a burst of energy because the opiate temporarily medicates conditions such as anxiety and depression.

The Drug Policy Alliance does an excellent job on its website of explaining the heroin we see here in the U.S. (www.drugpolicy.org/drug-facts/heroin-facts):

> *Street heroin is rarely pure and may range from a white to dark brown powder of varying consistency. Such differences typically reflect the impurities remaining from the manufacturing process and/or the presence of additional substances. These "cuts" are often sugar, starch, powdered milk and occasionally other drugs, which are added to provide filler.*

In my case, I was using what is known as black tar heroin, a sticky substance manufactured in Mexico that is less potent than East Coast Powder, or ECP. Tar heroin is generally injected or smoked on foil, while ECP can be easily snorted. Tar heroin has the reputation of being full of impurities; ECP is considered more pure. I personally encountered street heroin cut with substances such as instant coffee. One of the only public health advantages of tar is that it cannot easily be cut with fentanyl, a synthetic opioid that caused the deaths of thousands of users when dealers hoping to boost profits added it to heroin to cause a more intense "rush."

Today, heroin is less expensive, easier to find, and more potent than when I was using it. An inexperienced user can easily spend less than the price of a mixed drink to get a high so powerful it can be fatal. Add in a few drinks or a Xanax or Valium, and it is easy to spend less than you would on popcorn and a movie to have a whole night of intense sedation. Because of what is known as "tolerance," heroin creates diminishing returns. A user who may have been satisfied with one dose every eight to twelve hours may eventually find that the same dose doesn't last, creating unpleasant withdrawal symptoms. The more a person uses, the more he or she needs to use on a daily basis to achieve the same high. Eventually, it can cost hundreds of dollars per day to support a habit. At the peak of my using, I was spending $100 a day on drugs. While the vast majority of opioid users work or use legal means to pay for their drugs, some may turn to the street economy to support their addiction. This may include small-time dealing, theft, credit card fraud, and sex work. Because of the illegal nature of the heroin, it has a tendency to lure users away from mainstream economic activity.

Not all people who try heroin will become addicted, but it certainly is a slippery slope. There are many factors that influence who becomes addicted, such as family background, societal pressures, a history of trauma, and issues with mental illness. There are also many users who report none of these issues. Experimentation can lead to periods of abuse. If you suspect a friend or loved one is abusing heroin, my best advice is to listen without judgment. The stigma associated with heroin use creates a sense of isolation. Creating a sense of connection is a great bridge toward recovery. While it may be hard not to offer advice, early conversations can reaffirm your care and concern for this person. In the end, a user is just a person worthy of love and compassion who needs to be reassured there is still another way to live.

HIDDEN IN PLAIN SIGHT

It is painful enough to have a loved one addicted to any drug. That pain can be compounded when the drug is heroin. Heroin addiction does not just drive users into isolation. It can also push them into a circle of fear with little support from the community at large. My mother was forced to deal with her pain privately. In a place like West Chester, Ohio, in the '90s, heroin use would have been unfathomable to people in her social circle. People certainly knew I was missing from family events. My mother was unable to brag about any accomplishments of mine. During one period, she was only able to track my whereabouts through hospital bills and collect calls from jail.

According to the National Survey on Drug Use and Health (NSDUH) conducted by the Substance Abuse and Mental Health Services Administration, in 2012 an estimated 23.1 million Americans (8.9 percent) needed treatment for a problem related to drugs or alcohol, but only about 2.5 million people (1 percent) received treatment at a specialty facility. This means that the vast majority of users who are trying to get clean are dealing with detoxification and early recovery only with the aid of loved ones. This puts a huge burden on the caregivers when, in the case of heroin in particular, a treatment failure can lead to death.

Heroin users go through an intense three- to five-day withdrawal process during which they can become incapacitated. Symptoms may include abdominal cramping, diarrhea, restless legs, nausea, vomiting, anxiety, and sleeplessness. Family members may be called on to do everything from mortgaging their home to pay for treatment to hiding their adult children from drug dealers. The desperate situation is compounded by the sheer lack of information available on the topic. How could this be my child? Where did my brother get heroin? How could I have missed the signs?

After the short-term detox process, there can be a period of extended depression and hopelessness known as PAWS (post-acute withdrawal syndrome). When someone contacts me for help, I attempt to break all the medical explanations down to simple terms: When a person is using heroin, a great deal of his happy chemicals are coming from an outside source. Over time, the body slows production of its own happy chemicals in reaction to this outside source. When a user stops taking the outside source, it takes time for the body to build that production back up. Kicking heroin makes a user feel like her lover has left her and her best friend has died at the same time. The end of heroin use really feels like the death of a relationship. Your life has become consumed with this drug. It takes time to feel better, to feel anything. This can be difficult for loved ones who can interpret depression or anxiety as a lack of gratitude, motivation, or desire to stop using. The user may not have the ability, in the early stages, to feel many emotions other than primal ones, such as anger. Give it time.

In the past eighty years, AA, Alcoholics Anonymous, has made tremendous headway in normalizing the way people think about problem drinking. There has not been such a movement for the heroin user. But in growing numbers, families are creating their own support networks. Many of these were created as a way of making the death of a loved one have some kind of meaning. Social media is full of open and closed support groups with grieving families seeking someone who understands their experience. Groups like Northern Kentucky Hates Heroin (http://nkyhatesheroin .com) and the Davis Direction Foundation (http://davis directionfoundation.org) provide a place where parents can share information, receive support, and find resources. In addition to providing support for individuals, these groups have been instrumental in influencing state-level policies that impact users. Mothers and fathers are no longer afraid to sit on the stairs of their state capitol buildings or outside their congressperson's office, clutching a photo of their son or daughter who died as a result of an overdose. Policies are being changed, laws are being enacted, and the veil of silence is being broken.

HOW TO GET HELP:
THE FIRST STEPS OF RECOVERY

Recovery starts with a decision—one worth validating. To help people understand others with addiction problems and how to motivate them, researchers Carlo C. DiClemente and J. O. Prochaska introduced a six-stage model of change: precontemplation, contemplation, determination, action, maintenance, and termination or potential relapse. When a person gets to the point where he finally realizes it is time to stop—the determination stage—he has made huge progress, even if he falls back into an earlier stage. Heroin recovery is frequently a messy process that rarely results in the user getting clean forever the first time he is motivated to stop. However, with some support and encouragement it is possible to make the trajectory to long-lasting recovery a smoother one.

Breaking free from heroin is complicated at first, beginning with the painful three- to five-day withdrawal process. Many times I have heard loved ones ask, "Why don't they just stop?" This is easier said than done. Imagine figuring out how to schedule yourself for the flu. How can you take the time off work? Who will take care of your children? Who will help you when/if you are unable to care for yourself? Where is a safe place for this to happen, with twenty-four-hour access to both a bathroom and a shower? What are the things you need to alleviate your suffering? Can you afford these things having spent all your money or at least all of your disposable income on heroin? The tasks that need to be completed just to begin a journey to recovery can seem overwhelming.

Formulating a plan is the best way to be successful. Gather your tools and your support. There are some over-the-counter remedies such as loperamide and diphenhydramine that may help if a person has no insurance or plans to "kick" at home. For a person with access to medical care, a doctor may prescribe anything from gabapentin to a limited script of a benzodiazepine for sleep. You may also be referred to a substance abuse specialist since your practitioner may not have the legal ability to prescribe any kind of opioid replacement medication.

The Substance Abuse and Mental Health Services Administration (SAMHSA) has created tools that anyone seeking a program can access. The first one is a general treatment locator on SAMHSA's website at https://findtreatment .samhsa.gov, where you can find program information as well as phone numbers and addresses. SAMHSA also provides a comprehensive list of those providers who offer medication-assisted treatment (MAT) for substance abuse disorders at http://dpt2.samhsa.gov/treatment/directory.aspx.

If you or your loved one has some form of private insurance, call your plan administrator to see what your plan covers. Some people are completely unaware that their insurance covers MAT interventions such as buprenorphine until they call. Most plans have a preferred or required set of providers. This may require waiting for an opening, which can be extremely frustrating when a heroin user is motivated to receive treatment now.

With public insurance like Medicare or Medicaid, a person seeking treatment may need to contact individual sites to see what forms of insurance are accepted. With the passing of the Affordable Care Act, otherwise known as Obamacare, access to services was expanded. Unfortunately, many individual states took a pass on expanding Medicaid, leaving hundreds of thousands of Americans with limited resources still without coverage.

If a user is without any kind of insurance, there are some low-cost and no-cost options scattered across communities. Some residential treatment programs have scholarship programs. Most opioid replacement therapy clinics have private pay options for as low as $15 a day. This may seem high, but it's low in comparison to the $50 or $100 a day that's required to support a heroin habit. There are free support groups such as SMART Recovery (http://SMARTRecovery.org), LifeRing Secular Recovery (http://lifering.org), and 12step.org. Users may also find support through their local churches.

The news is not all dire. In fact, there is some very good news. Gene Heyman (http://geneheyman.com/books.htm), a research psychologist at McLean Hospital in Massachusetts, found that between 60 and 80 percent of people who were addicted to illicit drugs in their younger years were free by their thirties. In fact, most people who quit drugs do it on their own. I like to use the expression "five days to freedom." If you can dedicate five days to kicking, that is the first step to rebuilding your life. I kicked heroin cold turkey—completely unmedicated—in jail. I survived the worst-case scenario for detox. Then I stayed clean. The most important thing is finding someone to talk with, creating a plan, and believing you *can* stop using heroin. The research proves it.

THE MOST DANGEROUS TIME

When I started my process of recovery, I couldn't imagine that I would never use drugs again. If this had been suggested to me out loud, I might have laughed at the idea. Not because I didn't want this for myself. I simply did not feel I was capable of such a task. After getting out of jail many times before, I had started using again within a few hours. Fortunately, that last time I was transported directly to rehab, with no chance of finding my old friends in between. As I completed my rehab stay, I was surprised by just how many people I knew who had left rehab only to overdose and die. It wasn't just those who "split" or left the program before their time was completed. Over and over, it was a sad refrain. I constantly wondered, *Why is this happening?* When I got involved in harm reduction in 1999, I started to get answers.

Statistically, the most dangerous time for heroin users is after periods of abstinence. This includes incarceration, trips to rehab, extended hospital stays, and voluntary attempts to curb use. After periods of not using drugs, the body experiences a drop in tolerance. The same amount that a user was ingesting a few days, weeks, or months earlier is now potentially fatal. Compounding the risk is the fact that users may be too ashamed to admit to cravings when there is an expectation of sobriety. They may be using alone or in a location where they are less likely to receive any assistance if they overdose. While saying "Just don't use" is good in theory, falling short can be fatal. Instead, users need to be educated on their risk of overdose, as well as provided with naloxone.

What is naloxone (also known as Narcan)? The Harm Reduction Coalition describes it as an "opioid antagonist;"

that is, it's used to counter the effects of an opioid. Specifically, during an opioid overdose naloxone can be used to counteract life-threatening depression of the central nervous system and respiratory system, allowing the victim to breathe normally. Naloxone is a non-scheduled (or non-addictive) prescription medication. It only works if a person has opioids in her system.

Naloxone is an important tool in preventing overdose deaths, but it is not just for medical providers. It's being used every day by so-called laypersons or non-medical individuals trained to administer the drug to friends, loved ones, or even strangers in the event of an opioid overdose. In a report titled "Opioid Overdose Prevention Programs Providing Naloxone to Laypersons—United States, 2014" (Davidson, et al.), published in June 2015 by the Centers for Disease Control and Prevention (CDC), the authors reported:

> *Providing naloxone kits to laypersons reduces overdose deaths, is safe, and is cost-effective. U.S. and international health organizations recommend providing naloxone kits to laypersons who might witness an opioid overdose, to patients in substance use treatment programs, to persons leaving prison and jail, and as a component of responsible opioid prescribing.*

The report also shows that since the first harm reduction program began distributing naloxone to drug users and their friends and families in 1996, more than 150,000 people have been trained and provided with naloxone, which has resulted in over 26,000 overdose reversals nationally.

Most of the people who use their naloxone to revive someone are drug users themselves—the people most likely to
witness another person's overdose.

This may seem confusing. Why should I have naloxone
when I plan on staying clean? Why should I get naloxone
for my loved one when he is doing so well? Isn't naloxone
simply encouraging him to return to heroin use by providing him with a safety net? Naloxone is critical—again, a
person cannot get clean if he is dead. If we fully understand
that there's the slightest possibility that relapse will be part
of an individual's journey, then we should certainly be prepared for the very worst. In 2013, over 8,000 people died of
heroin overdoses in the U.S. One of the biggest contributing
factors is release from incarceration or treatment. Parents
who have lost a loved one to overdose are slowly becoming
the most vocal advocates in changing the laws that limit the
distribution of naloxone.

RECOVERY ESSENTIAL: WHAT IS MAT?

While twelve-step lingo has become a staple of the lexicon
in the United States, MAT, or medication-assisted treatment,
is much less familiar. Yet MAT is an important part of any
discussion about the treatment of heroin users. According to
SAMHSA, MAT "is the use of medications in combination
with counseling and behavioral therapies to provide a 'whole-
patient' approach to the treatment of substance use disorders."
MAT starts with the principle that medication can be a great
tool to assist patients in reaching their recovery goals. In the

case of heroin, continued use can come with considerable risks, including conditions like soft tissue infections known as abscesses; infection of the lining of the heart, known as endocarditis; hepatitis C; HIV; and overdose. Starting MAT can provide a bridge back to a healthy life.

Two of the most common forms of MAT are methadone and buprenorphine. These long-lasting opioid replacement medications are taken orally on a daily basis to ease withdrawal symptoms, reduce or eliminate cravings, block the impact of shorter-acting opioids like heroin, and create a routine of normalcy without procuring and ingesting illicit substances on a daily basis. By filling up the opiate receptors of the brain, the patient no longer experiences the ups and downs of addiction. Some opiate replacement patients report that these medications have the additional benefit of acting as mild antidepressants. On a therapeutic dose, the patient feels "normal." At a higher dose, opioid replacement medications also make it hard to "feel" shorter-acting opioids—again, like heroin.

After stabilizing on their dose of methadone or buprenorphine, the vast majority of users discontinue use of other opioids. Some users even find that MAT relieves their physical cravings from day one. I have heard patients describe this feeling as being like a miracle. This is not to say that these drugs are not without unpleasant side effects. With opioid replacement medications, there can be an elongated withdrawal process if the person is not tapered off the medication. There can be sedation, constipation, and excessive sweating. However, at a therapeutic dose and with close monitoring, an MAT patient can resume the activities of daily living.

Another form of MAT is oral or injected naltrexone. Unlike buprenorphine and methadone, which partially or fully fill the opiate receptor site, naltrexone blocks the effects of drugs such as opioids and alcohol. In other words, it takes the rewards out of using these drugs. Vivitrol is a time-release, injectable form of naltrexone that can last up to twenty-eight days. "The shot," as it is called, has become popular with criminal justice programs and parents who are concerned about what will happen when a heroin user reenters the community after jail and rehab. Of course, "the shot" is not without its own set of drawbacks. The main one is a high risk of overdose death after the shot reaches the end of the cycle. Others include issues with depression, being unable to taste food, and infections at the injection site.

I had positive experiences with MAT in my early attempts to quit heroin. While I did not stay off, it was no fault of the methadone. It was more an indication of my lack of support and the negative experiences I had that were related to the clinic environment. Because opiate use holds so much stigma, MAT sites are frequently located in undesirable areas or on the outskirts of the city. In addition, my MAT did not include the intensive counseling I would later receive in residential treatment. The rules around receiving MAT vary from location to location. Some programs that provide MAT require strict drug testing and counseling as a condition for receiving the medication, while others may only require drug testing. Anyone considering MAT should first look into the specific requirements of the program.

Despite being evidence-based, MAT is not without its controversy. Some recovery communities consider MAT a "crutch." There is special value placed on those who can do it on their own. Twelve-step, in particular, is built around the concept of "abstinence from all drugs." What if these drugs are lifesaving medications? For those who use MAT, they are often told they are still in active addiction. Twelve-step literature clearly states, "The only requirement for membership is a desire to stop using," yet those on MAT may feel like outsiders. They may even be encouraged to lower or stop their doses, discontinue their treatment, or even be forbidden to share or speak at meetings.

Recovery can be a long process with or without MAT. Anyone who is seeking treatment for heroin addiction should consider all the options. I made up my mind that I would try rehab. If that didn't work, I was going to go back on methadone. I had thought that even if I spent my life on methadone, it would certainly be better than sticking syringes in the soles of my feet. MAT, while not for everyone, should certainly be a consideration for those struggling to stay off heroin.

GENDER DIFFERENCES

When I am asked what the biggest barriers were early in my sobriety, I say being female is near the top of my list. In early recovery, it seemed as if everything was designed without any thought of the particulars of a woman's specific issues. I had questions, many questions, about everything from the return of my period to how a person comes to terms with having engaged in "survival sex"—trading sex for drugs. In addition, many women I knew in treatment were dealing with the loss of their children to "the system." Gender differences between men and women with substance abuse issues have been well researched in the past twenty years. Unfortunately, the treatment system has been slow to respond.

In a report prepared for clinical psychiatrists in 1999, Kathleen Brady and Carrie L. Randall outlined many of the factors that impact women and girls who use substances. They found that women typically begin using substances later in life than men, and are strongly influenced by spouses or boyfriends to use. This was true in my case: I was encouraged to use heroin for the first time by a male friend who was a seasoned user. The research found women and girls report different reasons for maintaining substance use. Many women, as I did, use drugs as a form of self-medication for conditions such as depression and anxiety. Dr. Brady and Dr. Randall also discovered that women tend to enter treatment sooner than men do. I was happy to be part of that statistic. At twenty-eight years old, I was one of the youngest clients out of nearly one hundred people in residential treatment. This made it challenging to find a peer group I could bond with until I was able to expand my support system outside of the treatment environment.

There is also significant stigma attached to being a woman with a drug problem. Women are seen as mothers and caregivers, capable of carrying a greater burden in society. When a woman acknowledges that she needs assistance, she is not measuring up to the impossible standards of femininity frequently portrayed in the media. It's seen as some kind of failure on her part. One can wonder whether, in response to these stressors in recent years, women have developed an increasing share of the epidemic of prescription opiate use. Since they are given in a medical setting, these highly abusable medications are often seen as an acceptable alternative to street drugs. As a direct result, overdose death rates among females are quickly rising.

For women who do decide they're ready to seek help, there may be barriers to finding care that is responsive to their unique needs. With nearly twice as many men using substances, there is frequently disparity in resources. In the treatment facility I attended, there were four male beds for every one female bed. In my experience, the program was based almost entirely on the medical model, a cookie-cutter approach that is still prevalent and manifests as a top-down approach in which addiction is discussed in terms of a "disease." This can be problematic for women whose substance abuse is a response to domestic violence, sexual abuse, or childhood trauma. Not only do the women feel diseased or broken, they may also find it impossible to trust staff members who hold positions of authority over them, without understanding their history of trauma.

In a 2009 report, "Substance Abuse Treatment: Addressing the Specific Needs of Women" (http://www.ncbi .nlm.nih.gov/books/NBK83252/), the Center for Substance Abuse Treatment (CSAT) recommends that "programs should ensure that all counseling activities are conducted in a respectful and caring manner and should not use counseling approaches that are contraindicated for trauma survivors." This type of treatment may be difficult to find in a sea of twenty-eight-day "spin dry" rehabs. I have seen women come to me in tears after being confronted in counseling sessions. I have been told of group activities that led to women being publicly shamed by their peers. In my treatment center, we were told the center was a "house," yet the "brothers" were frequently sexually aggressive. Trauma survivors may have a tough time building their self-esteem when they are being consistently triggered by predatory behavior from their fellow male residents.

For those who are lucky enough to find responsive care, the next barrier for women comes when they are attempting to get on their feet financially. Women need jobs as part of their rehabilitation process in order to achieve lasting recovery. The CSAT found evidence that "gainful employment can be a protective influence for preventing relapse," especially because they often have dependent children or other family members to support. In my rehab experience, men quickly found higher-paying jobs in the construction trades or information technology, whereas women were mostly only able to find jobs in the lower-paying retail or food service industries. Women need more job training, and they also need treatment that allows them to care for their children.

While "trauma-informed care" and treatment that is gender responsive are becoming more popular, we have a long way to go. Many of the recommendations presented decades ago are still not fully realized in our treatment system. Breaking away from "one size fits all" and into an approach that supports the needs of individuals is the next great step in achieving parity for women in need of substance abuse intervention.

INJURY AND ILLNESS

Getting off heroin is scary. The last thing a person wants to worry about is an illness or injury sabotaging her hard work. One of the most common areas of concern I hear after a person has stopped using heroin for a period of time is the use of pain medication. What will happen to me if I need to get a tooth pulled? If I need surgery? If I am in an accident? Will this derail what I have built? It is a rational fear. Getting free of heroin may have been the hardest challenge the person ever faced. The detox, the depression, and the stigma are all brutal. Finally you feel as if you are on the right path. Once you feel confident enough to learn the needle won't randomly slip into your arm or the straw accidentally go up your nose, it may be frightening to think that someday opioids may enter your body again. Medical issues are particularly scary because it feels as if you have limited choices.

Once you reach the other side, where you finally feel somewhat normal and perhaps even content without heroin, having a plan for potential traps is critical. *You* have to be your best advocate. If you are supporting a loved one, you may have to speak up for them. When I was a heroin user, I took the drugs orally, I snorted them, and I injected them without question. I put all my faith into the idea that whatever was in that plastic bag was going to make me feel better, even though that complete faith nearly killed me many times. The same blind faith can be applied to receiving medical treatment. Doctors seem like the ultimate authorities. But it is *your* body, *your* recovery. It is entirely okay to question whether a procedure or medication is necessary.

That doesn't make you a problem patient—it makes you an educated one. It makes you a person capable of making informed choices.

In a medical crisis, pain medicine may be necessary. The issue comes when we once again notice the shift in tolerance and our mood as related to the intake of these medications. Any doctor who prescribes these medications knows they can treat your pain. But he may not be fully aware of the fact that you have a history of using opioids. That distinction can be challenging to vocalize. Users fear that if they tell their health care provider of their history of addiction, they will experience discrimination and will be given less than what is necessary for pain management. On the other hand, in a case like mine where the doctor did not check my addiction history, the patient can be handed an excess of medication that creates the potential for refueling addictive tendencies.

I have been prescribed pain medication numerous times in my recovery. The first time was for my miscarriage. I received pain medicines with all three of my C-sections. The last time was for an abscessed tooth. While I experienced discomfort with the process of getting off these opioids, there was never a moment when I thought to myself: *This makes me want to get heroin.* I was well supported, well prepared, and honest with both my doctor and myself. There is also growing research that shows alternating ibuprofen and acetaminophen in the three days after surgery can be more effective than opioids in reducing the pain of many procedures. I found this to be true with my last surgery. I had assumed a person who had ingested two grams a day of heroin would

get no help from over-the-counter medications. I was pleas-
antly surprised that this is not the case.

If you *need* medication, by all means take it. Be aware
of how you can recognize any cravings, irritability, or withdrawal symptoms. Make a plan for managing your medication without abusing it. I asked myself every time I took
the medicine: Do I need this? How am I feeling? How is my
pain? If I feel uncomfortable, can I check in with someone
to let her know I am taking this medicine? Know yourself,
know your body, and ask questions. Be your own advocate.
Only *you* know what you need. Communicate this to your
providers.

THE PAST SHOULDN'T DICTATE MY FUTURE

I used to use heroin. I used to use heroin every day. I used to
inject heroin. I used to inject it into my feet, my legs, my fingers. I lost everything—no, I gave up everything for heroin.
These things are so easy for me to say now. I can type them.
I can email you about them. I can show you pictures. I can
even forget about them for a little while. I can go most of
the day, part of a week, or a long string of moments without
remembering I was once a hardcore heroin user.

Something always brings me back to that place. I am not
just Tracey. I remember that I am Tracey, who used to use heroin. I might be reaching for the phone at work: I glance down.
I notice the scar on my forearm. I might be on the train: I see
someone nodding off in the corner. I might wake up in the
morning with swollen hands, as when I used to inject drugs

into my fingers. I walk past the police: I remember those times when I needed to avert my glance. I see sugar or dried creamer or even salt spilled on the counter: I slowly laugh at myself. I am different from others, I tell myself. Heroin use has subtly, irrevocably altered my worldview.

There comes a point when every former user must decide how much to disclose about herself. Should I tell people? Whom do I tell? What would happen if I did tell them? Will they reject me? Will they hold it against me for a lifetime? Will I always be that woman/man who used to do heroin? There are no easy answers. Some people feel that the first step in receiving help is admitting to others that they use heroin. This can be done anonymously in an Internet forum. It can be to a service provider. It can be to a close friend, relative, or even an acquaintance. Heroin, of all drugs, holds so much stigma. This admission can hold serious repercussions. I receive anonymous messages where people disclose, "I am worried about losing my family." Or it could be a job, or housing, or their children. The admission holds so much power. It can be important to admit that you need help. But be aware that everyone you tell may not be forgiving.

After periods of abstinence, the question then arises: Should I tell people I am an addict? I just met this man/woman or I just applied for this job or I just decided to reconnect with my family. I can only suggest things that worked for me, like creating a checklist for yourself. What are my reasons for telling this person? Is there a medical reason I need to tell him, like having hepatitis C or HIV and planning to be intimate? Are you planning to rely on this person for support? How vulnerable are you? Would you be able to handle rejection?

We don't need to lie or mislead. We also don't need to immediately volunteer information. Imagine a job interview that started with "Hi, I am John. I used to be a heroin addict. Please trust me." Or, on a date, when you discuss your history of abscesses over appetizers. Perhaps the family reunion can print up some T-shirts that announce, JOHN JUST GOT BACK FROM REHAB. In other words, a user needs to be in charge of his or her own history. Just as with any other medical information, use some discretion. Not because you should be ashamed. Quite the contrary. You should be wary of telling others because what you have accomplished is precious. It is something that may not be understood by everyone. Once that information is out there, you have no control over the outcome. Just be prepared for any outcome, both negative and positive.

After years of being off heroin, you may find you no longer identify with the term "addict," "user," or "junkie." That is perfectly acceptable. The past should not dictate the future. Just be aware that some people find a power in connection. They enjoy using a common vernacular to explain their experience. Some days I use "recovering addict." Other days I call myself a junkie. Most days I call myself a mother, a wife, and a friend. These things are not all mutually exclusive. They make me proud of who I am today.

THE BURDENS OF THE PAST

There was one night in the mid-90s when I was fumbling through my belongings in my shopping cart underneath the streetlight in the alley where I was essentially living at the time. As I folded one of my dirty shirts, I thought to myself, *I am going to go back to school one day*. This would seem completely incongruent with my circumstances at that time. Where would I even start? I didn't know where my life would take me. I only knew where I wanted to go. My goals were a spark for my recovery. The loss of hope keeps people stuck doing the same things, getting the same results. Developing a goal was one of the things I did early on that took the needle out of my arm.

Unfortunately for me, I was a convicted felon. My felony conviction: "sales/transport of a controlled substance." My whole future was sidelined by a $20 bag of drugs. Initially, as a convicted felon on probation I had no civil rights. I had no right to vote. The police had the right to search my home, my vehicle, or my person at any time without probable cause. I could be denied everything from federal financial aid for college to public assistance to the ability to live in any type of Section 8 low-income housing. These are all serious blows to a person coming out of jail with no money, no place to live, and the vast majority of employers unwilling to take a chance on employing her.

For the ex-offender, the road to recovery can be an uphill battle, but it is well worth the journey. The alternative is often a revolving door of incarceration and extended relapse.

Many ex-offenders may be unaware that once they complete some type of rehabilitation program, they may again become eligible to utilize public services. In my case, I was able to enter college through an ex-offender program called Project Rebound. They wrote a letter to the school to negotiate my admissions despite my low GPA. Many such programs exist around the country, some occupying spaces in student resource centers.

There are also job reentry services designed to help those in recovery find employment if they have criminal records. Finding a job is especially critical, because having meaningful activity in daily life is an integral part of recovery. Yet the National Institute of Justice found that a criminal record reduced the likelihood of a job offer or even a callback by nearly 50 percent. Job reentry programs can help with important things like securing identification, writing a resumé, obtaining clothes for an interview, and getting substance abuse counseling, housing referrals, and job leads. I applied for my first job in recovery by tapping into a program that actively solicited companies willing to hire ex-offenders for job openings. With the help of job coaching I received through the program, I was confident enough to explain my felony in the interview. I got that job, which led to an even better job as a counselor. Small steps on my part ended up leading to huge gains.

Ex-offenders with drug problems may find additional pressures when they return to the community. When I was released from treatment, I had to decide whether I was strong enough to move back to my old "stomping grounds." In reality, that area was the only place I could afford. It was one block from where I used to buy my drugs. Drugs and violence were constant reminders outside my door. I wasn't the only one. There was another halfway house for parolees located two blocks from me. To visit my probation officer, I had to walk through the open-air drug market; the only other option would have required traveling thirty minutes out of my way. These were tough situations to manage for someone with very little recovery under her belt. Similar triggers can occur if the person in recovery moves in with family. Using buddies and dealers can still be just around the corner. Experiencing the additional stress of feeling trapped is not uncommon when drug testing is a condition of probation or parole, even though the person is living on the outside.

WILL I EVER USE AGAIN?

There is no question that there is hope for those trying to stop heroin. Every day across the United States, users gather their courage, as well as their over-the-counter remedies. They call detox centers. They find out their prayers are answered: A bed has become available. They pack their bag for rehab facilities. They drive miles from their home in the dark to be the first one in line for their appointment at the methadone clinic. They walk slowly, scared and ashamed, next to their mother or father into a doctor's office. Their hopes are high, their expectations are low. They have become desperate after months of sleepless nights wondering if this day would ever come. The time for action is now. Recovery, in whatever form it takes, begins with a step into the unknown. What comes next is chaotic at first. It is painful. It is beautiful. It is living, not existing. It is perfect in all its imperfections. Life falls into a rhythm, until one day heroin is no longer the first thing you crave. It will be the last thing you want to remember.

Through my personal life, in my work, and in my advocacy I have seen the most hopeless of users get off heroin. I have also seen them stay off. There isn't a week that goes by when I don't get a message saying, "Remember me?" followed by a few lines about their story. It's been estimated that over four million people have tried heroin. Yet the vast majority of these people are not using today. Whether they "aged out," used MAT, found religion, tried meetings, went to rehab, or simply stopped on their own, the numbers don't lie. There is more than just hope that a person can quit: There is evidence. Like the users who never touched heroin after returning to the U.S. from Vietnam, even a change in environment can lead to a life free of heroin.

Will I ever use again? The research is certainly on my side. A study published in 2007 by M.L. Dennis, M.A. Foss, and C.K. Scott with eight years of data from more than 1,100 users found that for those who achieve a year of sobriety, fewer than half relapse. If you can make it to five years of sobriety, your chance of relapse is less than 15 percent. After many years of stable abstinence, there are those who will choose to return to social drinking. Others might choose to use cannabis. That isn't my particular path. While I don't believe that ingesting these substances automatically opens the door to a return to heroin or other drugs, it isn't the path for me. When I think of drinking, I ask myself, *Will this enhance my life in some way?* The answer is always no.

To maintain a life free of heroin, I customized a familiar list of recommendations. The first thing I did was develop a strong system of social support. This included my family, my groups, and friends who were clean and sober. The second factor was obtaining stable affordable housing. The third factor was finding employment that was flexible enough to maintain my schedule of supportive activities. The fourth was finding productive activities I loved, including school and volunteer work. The final and critical element was gaining some insight into the reasons I started using drugs, so I could find new ways of coping. This came in the form of journaling, guided recovery worksheets, and individual sessions with a therapist. While replacement meds and antidepressants were not part of my individual story, they may also be a necessary tool. Although every person kicking the habit may not be able to do everything on this list, research shows that each of these things can increase your chances of success.

Will I ever use again? I say the answer is no. I work every day to make the distance a little farther between the needle and myself.

REFERENCES

Davidson, Peter J., Michael K. Gilbert, Stephen Jones and Eliza Wheeler. "Opioid Overdose Prevention Programs Providing Naloxone to Laypersons—United States, 2014." Centers for Disease Control and Prevention, *Morbidity and Mortality Weekly*. June 2015. http://www.cdc.gov/mmwr/preview/mmwrhtml/mm6423a2.htm

Including:
a. Doyon, S., S.E. Aks, and S. Schaeffer. "Expanding Access to Naloxone in the United States." *Clin Toxicol (Phila)* 52 (2014): 989–92.
b. Walley, A., Z. Xuan, H.H. Hackman, et al. "Opioid Overdose Rates and Implementation of Overdose Education and Nasal Naloxone Distribution in Massachusetts: Interrupted Time Series Analysis." *BMJ* 346 (2013): 1–12.

c. World Health Organization. "Community Management of Opioid Overdose." Geneva, Switzerland: World Health Organization, 2014.
d. Coffin, P.O. and S.D. Sullivan. "Cost-effectiveness of Distributing Naloxone to Heroin Users for Lay Overdose Reversal." *Ann Intern Med* 158 (2013): 1–9.
e. Substance Abuse and Mental Health Services Administration. "Opioid Overdose Prevention Toolkit." Rockville, MD: Substance Abuse and Mental Health Services Administration, 2014. Available at http://store.samhsa.gov/product/Opioid-Overdose-Prevention-Toolkit-Updated-2014/SMA14-4742.

Substance Abuse and Mental Health Services Administration. "Medication and Counseling Treatment," September 2015. http://www.samhsa.gov/medication-assisted-treatment/treatment.

Brady, Kathleen T.; Randall, Carrie L., Psychiatric Clinics of North America, Volume 22, Issue 2. "Gender Differences in Substance Use Disorders," June 1999.

Dennis, Michael L., Foss, Mark A., Grella, Christine E., Scott, Christy K. 2007 UCLA Integrated Substance Abuse Programs, "Gender Similarities and Differences in the Treatment, Relapse, and Recovery Cycle," February 2008.

ACKNOWLEDGMENTS

There are many people I want to thank for helping to make this book possible. Thanks to my family for supporting me, especially my husband Christian and our three children. Thank you to the wonderful team that believed in me and my message: Stephanie Knapp, Editor; Tabitha Lahr, Interior Design & Production Editor; Tim Green of Faceout Studio, Cover Design; Lori Kranz, Proofreader; Holly Cooper, Copyeditor; Donna Galassi, Marketing Director; Molly Conway; and Susan Weinberg. To my fabulous agent Lynn Johnston who believed in me from day one, Suzanne Williams, and the entire team at Seal Press and Perseus Books. Thanks to Debi Alley, Jason Norelli, Paul Dertien, Jen P. Bixler, the Sept 2007 moms, The She Wolves, Ron, my writing group including Teddie Honey and Justin Tyler Hughes, Ali Onder, Guilherme Borges da Costa, my workplace support system, my Reddit friends, Dr. Don Teater, Eliza Wheele, and the people, both alive and dead, who believed in me when I couldn't believe in myself.

ABOUT THE AUTHOR

Michael Kerner

Tracey Helton Mitchell is a recovering heroin addict. After completing rehab in 1998, she dedicated her life to the care and treatment of heroin users. Tracey entered school through an ex-offender's program where she earned a bachelors of business administration and masters of public administration. In addition, she is a certified addiction specialist and supervisor. She was featured in the documentary *Black Tar Heroin: The Dark End of the Street*. She has also been featured by *CNN, Anderson Cooper, Vice, The Huffington Post,* and *The New York Times*. Tracey lives in the San Francisco Bay Area with her husband and three children.

SELECTED TITLES FROM SEAL PRESS

Loaded: Women and Addiction, by Jill Talbot. $17, 978-1-58005-2184. Part autobiography, part exposé, *Loaded: Women and Addiction* weaves Talbot's own battles with addiction with various addiction stories of other women.

Something Spectacular: The True Story of One Rockette's Battle with Bulimia, by Greta Gleissner. $16, 978-1-58005-4157. The first book to give a voice to the pervasive but often unaddressed problem of eating disorders in the dance industry, *Something Spectacular* is a gripping exposé of the insidious nature of eating-related diseases—and a profound account of one woman's journey toward self-acceptance and recovery.

Shades of Blue: Writers on Depression, Suicide, and Feeling Blue, edited by Amy Ferris. $16, 978-1-58005-5956. The writers in *Shades of Blue* share real and unforgettable stories of their personal battles with depression, grief, and suicide, offering solidarity, and hope for all those who feel as if they're struggling alone.

The Drinking Diaries: Women Serve Their Stories Straight Up, edited by Caren Osten Gerszberkg and Leah Odze Epstein. $16, 978-1-58005-4119. Whether it's shame, sober sex, and relapsing, or college drinking, bonding, and comparing the benefits of pot vs. booze, *Drinking Diaries* is a candid look at the pleasures and pains of drinking, and the many ways in which it touches women's lives.

Riding Fury Home: A Memoir, by Chana Wilson. $17, 978-1-58005-4324. Exquisitely written and devastatingly honest, *Riding Fury Home* is a shattering account of one family's struggle against homophobia and mental illness—from the suffocating intolerance of the 50's through the liberation made possible by the women's movement in the 70's—and a powerful story of healing, forgiveness, and redemption.

She Bets Her Life: A True Story of Gambling Addiction, by Mary Sojourner. $18, 978-1-58005-2986. Sojourner's eloquence, openness, and talent for research provide keen insight and resources to help steer women with gambling addictions (and their loved ones) toward help and healing.

Find Seal Press Online
sealpress.com
@sealpress
Facebook | Twitter | Instagram | Tumblr | Pinterest